The Real Teflon Don

How An Elite Team of New York State Troopers Helped Take Down America's Most Powerful Mafia Family

by Matt Gryta
with George Karalus

Cazenovia Books
Buffalo (USA)

Published by Cazenovia Books, Buffalo, New York

Printed in the United States of America

ISBN 978-0-9749253-6-3

First Edition

"I will say emphatically that there is no Mafia in this country and no national crime syndicate."

—J. Edgar Hoover, 1961

Michael Corelone: My father's no different than any other powerful man – any man who's responsible for other people, like a senator or a president.

Kay: *[laughs]* You know how naïve you sound?

Michael: Why?

Kay: Senators and presidents don't have men killed.

Michael: Oh, who's being naïve, Kay?

—*The Godfather*

Contents

Introduction

This book chronicles the creation of a special investigative unit of the New York State Police Bureau of Criminal Investigation as an aftermath of the famed November 1957 State Police raid in Apalachin that revealed the existence of an organized nationwide crime network. The book also provides an overview of the empire of the Mafia's Real "Teflon Don," Stefano Magaddino, and examines the rich tapestry of the many underworld criminal activities that took place in Western New York directly or indirectly related to the team's work or as an aftermath of the highly successful and never disclosed undercover unit's work in the late 1960s and early 1970s.

The team of dedicated electronic warriors didn't call themselves the Forest Avenue Boys. That tag was added by their admirers many years later in recognition of their unique role in the unraveling of the Magaddino Empire. Meet the team.

Maury Gavin, a former South Buffalo, New York altar boy, joined the State Police in 1950 and was promoted to senior investigator in 1962, two years before the secret units were formed. Born Maurice D. Gavin, the co-leader of the Forest Avenue Boys died of a heart attack at the age of 75 in 2001 while working with Former Troopers Helping Hands. He got involved in the charity after his 1979 retirement, helping families cope with the terminal illnesses of their children. He frequently delivered spending money

1

to the homes of the families about to go with their dying children on wish trips set up by the organization. In keeping with Gavin's near-legendary compassion for others, there was only a memorial Mass for him at his favorite Roman Catholic Church in the Buffalo suburb of Orchard Park because there was no burial service. He had made arrangements to donate his body to the New York State University at Buffalo Medical School with the hope that his remains could lead to some discoveries that could aid the hundreds of terminally ill kids, most afflicted with cancer, he had befriended in retirement.

Norman Rivard, a French resistance fighter in World War II whose family migrated to New York City after the war, was a co-leader of the Boys. Rivard was a state trooper from Sept. 1, 1955 through Oct. 16, 1974, ending his career on the state Drug Enforcement Task Force before retiring to Florida with his wife.

Loren "Biddy" Bidwell, a former FBI agent, was a trooper from July 31, 1961 to December 31, 1970, retiring from Troop H.

Edward Pawlak was a state trooper from 1950 to 1973. His last unit was the Troop H Drug Enforcement Task Force. The Buffalo-born Pawlak went on to become security chief for the Harrison Radiator Division of General Motors on Aug. 1, 1973. A graduate of Buffalo's Seneca Vocational High School who attended the University of Buffalo, later to be known as the State University of New York at Buffalo, Pawlak was appointed to the Bureau of Criminal Investigation in 1958. He was promoted to the rank of investigator in 1959. In his last stint with the State Police, he was coordinator in charge of the Buffalo office of the State Police Special Investigations Unit which by then had become an arm of the state's Organized Crime Task Force. He now resides in St. Augustine, Florida.

George K. Karalus, after six years in the U.S. Marine Corps, graduated from the Troopers Academy in Albany, NY, in 1958. In May 1972, he was awarded a bachelor of science degree in both political science and American history from Niagara University in Lewiston, New York, not far from the Real Teflon Don's row of expensive houses. Karalus earned a master of science degree from Buffalo's Canisius College in 1974. After retiring from the state police, he worked as an investigator in the Erie County District Attorney's office. He also taught in the Williamsville, Cheektowaga-Sloan and Depew public school systems in the Buffalo suburbs and was a criminal justice instructor at Niagara University in the 1970s. Karalus, a baseball and basketball letter earner at Buffalo's Burgard Vocational High School, passed up a possible professional baseball career to go into the Marines. His ability to connect with Buffalo's street-level criminals both inside and outside the Mafia led to the discovery of Magaddino's "Cadillac Reef," the Delaware Park Lake burial ground for dozens of stolen vehicles which became part of the more than $350,000 in pre-inflation dollars of stolen property he played a major role in recovering.

Edward Palascak, born in Pennsylvania, first came to Western New York to work for Westinghouse which had a large operation in the Buffalo suburb of Tonawanda. After passing the State Troopers exam he was initially assigned to the force's Thruway Division, working his way up the ladder to investigator status. He ultimately retired to Largo, Florida.

Kenneth J. "Kenny" Troidl, known to his team members as "The Kid" because of his relative youth, was the master wiretap and bugging expert on the team. A trooper from 1962 until 1986, he later served as a key investigator for the New York State Inspector General's Office tracking down corruption in state government. He took an early retirement at age 51 in 1991. He was a member of the federal-state team that arrested the Real Teflon Don Magaddino on racketeering charges in 1968. "The Kid" took part in the Boys' successful and legal bugging of Johnny Sacco's Buffalo home. After his state service, he went on to work as a private investigator specializing in helping businesses fight industrial spying. Because of "The Kid's" wiretapping expertise, he played a major investigative role in a number of later Buffalo-area raids on illegal gambling operations. These included the summertime 1974 breakup of a major horse betting room that did close to $1.2 million in business annually in the Kenmore Towers Apartments north of Buffalo. Troidl was lauded at his retirement in September 1991 by then Erie County, NY, District Attorney Kevin M. Dillon as being "at the very top of the ladder in terms of conducting thorough investigations." State Supreme Court Justice Frederick M. Marshall, who the team relied upon for many of its ex parte bugging orders, said of Troidl that had he been a defense attorney and known Troidl had done the investigating on his client, he would know "my client is in trouble."

David Leroy was transferred to the team from Syracuse. He never grew fond of Buffalo. One night he heard a strange language on the Swiatek wire. He asked Karalus if he could speak and understand Portuguese, the language he assumed he was hearing. Karalus told him that was really Polish which Karalus was able to translate for him because Karalus had grown up in a largely Polish-American section of Buffalo, New York.

****

Court-ordered "live wires" or phone taps were placed in locations around Western New York where the mob conducted business.

Sam Pieri's kitchen was wired in October 1964. The Boys would listen to him yell at his wife until she left the house many days to get her hair done. Sam Pieri, who had immense power to get things done for Magaddino's boys, like clockwork most days would leave home at noon and return by 5 p.m. for supper. From the wires the Forest Avenue Boys knew that Pieri went to bed each night at 11 p.m.

Santasiero's restaurant at 1329 Niagara Street at Lafayette Avenue, the quintessential neighborhood spaghetti place in Buffalo, for decades was considered by residents of the city's West Side as a hidden local treasure and which was renowned for its "divine pasta fazool" served with hot peppers on the side. Magaddino's chiefs met daily there from noon to 3:30 p.m. Magaddino showed up there once at Christmas time in 1966 and his underlings kissed his hand as a sign of respect.

The Town Casino, once Buffalo's premier nightclub, was wired because Freddy Randacchio would frequently dine there along with many of his mob associates and local politicians he knew.

Introduction

The Club Thirty-One at Elmwood Avenue and Johnson Park was a renowned Buffalo restaurant opened by the DiGiulio brothers in 1942 and frequented by the area's top politicians, celebrities and Magaddino's boys.

Freddy Randaccio's home was not wired but the Forest Avenue Boys learned through its taps that Randaccio's long-time girlfriend from Buffalo's Riverside area pulled in $6000 doing tricks in New Orleans during the 1967 Mardi Gras season but had to give New Orleans cops $2000 of the take to be spared arrest.

Magaddino's home in Lewiston, New York and his Niagara Falls funeral parlor had wires the Boys inherited from the FBI and rather quickly realized were worthless because they had apparently been discovered by The Don's top officers who made sure nothing significant was discussed at those locations.

Tommy Chooch's restaurant on Richmond and Rhode Island was where Magaddino's chieftains came daily for breakfast and coffee. It proved to be one of the Boys' best taps.

At *Master burglar Brownie Swiatek's home* on Shanley Street, he and his associates could be heard discussing the jobs they had pulled off and were planning with mob permission.

Joe Fino's home in West Seneca proved to be a treasure trove of information on mob gambling operations.

The Blue Banner Social Club on Prospect Avenue was another hangout for Magaddino's top operatives.

Johnny Sacco could frequently be found at the *The Talisman supper club* on Hertel Avenue.

Buffalo City Hall was not wired but allowed for surveillance of mobsters like Jimmy LaDuca entering and leaving through its rear doors.

Wires in Niagara County, NY included at the *Lewiston home of Benjamin Nicolletti Sr.* and the *homes of Samuel "Sam the Farmer" Frangiamore and Police Capt. George Cruickshank.*

The Boys recorded the phone calls of Frankie "the Bugman" of Cleveland to "Sam" Pieri, Magaddino's connection to the Cleveland Mafia, who passed on the information for Sacco to set up shipments of stolen televisions from a Cheektowaga warehouse and about stolen golf balls and ladies hair permanent sets all of which

Introduction

the Forest Avenue Boys passed on to officials of the Pennsylvania State Police whom they trusted and which led to the seizures of all those shipments in 1968.

Like all of Magaddino's major burglary heists, the golf balls and permanent sets had been "sold" in advance to out of town crime associates and sometimes out of the country buyers, making their seizures extra traumatic for Magaddino's legions.

The Magaddino-controlled *Camellia Linen Supply Co. Inc.*, 460 East Delavan Avenue near a railroad overpass was run by Magaddino's wife-cheating son-in-law Jimmy LaDuca.

Adam's Como Lounge, 204 Como Park Boulevard, Cheektowaga, was one of that Buffalo's suburb's most expensive restaurants and a frequent stopping off point for the morally and criminally-suspect Cheektowaga police higher-ups whom the Elmwood Avenue Boys never trusted.

Anton's Restaurant at 2250 Walden Avenue at Union Road was another stop for criminally-suspect cops and mobsters and the burglar boys Swiatek and the Goose and their crowd.

Sisti Galleries and Art School was operated by boxer-turned-artist and art gallery owner Anthony "Tony" Sisti at 469 Franklin Street near Allen Street in the city's Bohemian Allentown District. Sisti was long suspected of being the Magaddino family's disposer of stolen artwork though he was never formally charged.

Panaro's Snowball Lounge and Restaurant owned by mob-connected Pasqual Panaro at 319 Hampshire Street was the site of a multi-agency raid on May 8, 1967 on the bachelor party of Joe "Lead Pipe Joe" Todaro's son, Joe Jr., which prompted a massive, but unsuccessful defamation suit by "Lead Pipe" Joe.

St. Anthony of Padua Church at 160 Court Street directly behind Buffalo City Hall was the spot where the Forest Avenue Boys would regularly witness Jimmy LaDuca entering City Hall for his meetings with Mayor Sedita's chief city lawyer and the site of the Boys game-playing with the minds of the less-than-Einsteinian LaDuca.

The Roseland Grill at 492 Rhode Island at Chenango Street.

The pay phone in front of Buffalo Police Headquarters.

Introduction

A pay phone near the Busti Fruit Market at 514 Busti near Jersey Street—a fruit store that was frequented by Magaddino associates taking advantage of what they apparently assumed was a nearby pay phone the authorities couldn't tap.

A Niagara Street pay phone on Austin Street was used by "Sam" Pieri to talk to Sam Rizzo about "6 for 5" monies linked to the loan sharking operation Pieri ran for Magaddino.

A Genesee Street pay phone at Buffalo's Schiller Park, often used by "Brownie" Swiatek and Carrie Rapp.

Carrie M. Rapp's "antique" shop on Buffalo's Broadway. ("The Fat Lady" who handled stolen property for Sacco and his gangs).

Sench Jewelers at 401 Fillmore Avenue near Memorial Drive (owned by Stanley J. Senchowa).

"Joe's Car Wash" in the 200 block of Niagara Street near both Buffalo Columbus Hospital at 300 Niagara and the famed Balistreri's Bakery at 307 Niagara—a frequent stop for Randacchio.

Mark's auto parts junkyard on William Street near Shanley Street in the Buffalo suburb of Sloan used by Magaddino's boys for their stolen car operations.

Kenmore Avenue Smoke Shop in Kenmore used by Bobby Bonner.

A public telephone in the Executive Hotel in the Buffalo suburb of Cheektowaga where many of Magaddino's higher ups liked to hang out.

Oliver Street Club in North Tonawanda, north of Buffalo, a gambling operation run by Bennie Nicholetti.

1. The Mother of All Raids

Stefano Magaddino, in addition to being one of the most bloodthirsty and violence-prone Old World-born Mafioso dons, also inadvertently became the Godfather of the New York State Police Special Investigations units which played a major role in the dismantling of an organized crime network the late J. Edgar Hoover only belatedly admitted had been thriving for decades under his watch.

It was Magaddino's decision to stage the historic November 1957 summit of the leadership of La Cosa Nostra at the 58-acre Central New York estate of one of his loyal underbosses, Joseph "The Barber" Barbara in Apalachin, New York. That decision cost the lives of several men who openly faulted the Niagara Falls, N. Y., undertaker afterward. Scorned for months after the raid, the Real Teflon Don put a stop to that intra-familia criticism by having "assignments" carried out on his loudest critics in the national organization and more particularly in his Western New York kingdom.

The November 1957 "summit" was partly the result of the killings in the late 1950s of several top mob figures involved in Mafia turf wars, including the daylight killing in a hotel barbershop of Albert Anastasia. That hit was reportedly approved by the Mafia's ruling Commission, which included Magaddino, and was carried out by hit men hired by Vito Genovese, head of New York City's Genovese family which was then the biggest operationally and allied with the Lucchese and Gambino arms of La Cosa Nostra. In the midst of what was looking like the start of a full blown, bloody war among New York City's five families and concerns about international narcotics, gambling and the prospects for "owning" elected officials nationwide at all levels of government and concerns about the overall command of the Mafia, powerful mob barons from across the country and from Italy arrived at the New York estate of Barbara, then a top Mafia baron helping control operations in southern central New York State and northeastern Pennsylvania.

Genovese wasn't the only powerful Mafia Don upset with word of Anastasia's attempts to grab a chunk of Don Santo G. Trafficante Jr.'s lucrative Havana casino operations. The international narcotics trade and the Cuban revenue stream from gambling and narcotics were scheduled to be major targets of discussion at the Apalachin session before it was cut short by pesky New York State troopers. Among the other topics up for debate would be the mob-controlled New York City garment industry and related loansharking operations.

Shortly before Apalachin got underway, representatives of Magaddino's Western New York family and the Detroit and Montreal families reportedly met with Sicilian Mafiosi at the Grand Hotel des Palmes in Palermo to solidify "business" connections. Magaddino played a central role in the agenda for that Sicilian meeting as well as the Apalachin summit. Magaddino had also hoped the "secret" Apalachin session would deal with growing rumors of Vito Genovese's spiraling desires to eliminate his powerful New York City rivals and the mob's "Commission" so that he could adopt the long-abandoned title of "boss of all bosses." But the haste in planning the details of the Apalachin "summit" played a major role in its embarrassing failure for the mob elite.

The arrests and later indictments of a handful of the several dozen "made men" who attended that confab prompted New York Gov. W. Averell Harriman to heed the advice of trusted aides to form New York State Police Special Investigation units such as the Forest Avenue Boys. Harriman's successor Nelson Rockefeller expanded their clandestine activities.

The successes of the New York State Police SIUs in generating legitimate information about organized crime activities continued until the Democrat-controlled Congress in the early

1970s, spooked by the Machiavellian antics of President Richard M. Nixon and the growing anti-Viet Nam War protests, gutted much of the nation's intelligence gathering capacities. Nixon's Watergate follies fed the Democrat paranoia about secret intelligence operations.

In November 1957 it was fortunate for Joe Barbara Jr., son of the Apalachin mob boss, that Magaddino—who had men killed for openly questioning his administration of the disastrous "summit"—did not learn that it had been the kid's ham-fisted handling of accommodations for some of the mobsters who came for the summit that set the law enforcement ball rolling against what came to be known as La Cosa Nostra.

It all started on Nov. 13, 1957. Joey Jr. was able to get bunks for his high-rolling mob pals at the Parkway Motel in nearby Vestal. That proved to be a big mistake. What began as a routine investigation and information-gathering effort stemming from the motel owner's complaint about a bad check, ended up turning Sgt. Edgar Croswell of the New York State Police Bureau of Criminal Investigation into "Apalachin Ed," a country cop who, though briefly trashed by some in the news media, went down in history as the "24-7" lawman who trapped and publicly exposed the Mafia and its higher ups.

What Croswell didn't know on the morning of Nov. 13, 1957 was that U.S. immigration officials had received a solid tip from an informant in Italy that a secret summit of the leaders of the American Mafia was in the works. But in just doing his job, Croswell ended up inflicting on the Mafia the most punishing blow it was to suffer after many decades of profitable, bloody and largely-ignored operations in the United States.

As Croswell and Investigator Vincent Vasisko were taking down information in the relatively new Vestal motel from one of its owners early on the afternoon of Nov. 13, 1957, Joey Barbara Jr. pulled into the motel's parking lot in one of his expensive cars. Croswell, a battle-hardened veteran lawman who had been eyeing the Barbara clan since the mid-1940s, pulled Vasisko into a sitting room off the lobby, telling him it was "Barbara's kid" and they ought to find out what he was doing at the motel. Joey B told the motel keeper he wanted to reserve three double rooms for two nights with the bill charged to the account of the Canada Dry Bottle Company of Endicott which his father operated. Croswell's suspicions increased when Joey B. refused to tell the motel owner who would be staying in the rooms, claiming his father was having a meeting of some of his Canada Dry associates and insisting he couldn't then say exactly who would be using the rooms. Joey B. left with three sets of room keys. Croswell told Vasisko "It looks like Joe's having a little pow-wow and maybe we'd better take a look at what's happening at the bottling plant."

For over a decade Croswell had been monitoring the elder Barbara because of reports he had been a suspect in three murders in Pennsylvania in the 1930s and rumors he was now the chief mobster in the south central part of New York State, operating the beer distributing and soft drink plant in Endicott as "cover." Croswell assumed, but couldn't prove that the large shipments of sugar to Barbara's Endicott plan were actually being used in the production of bootleg whiskey sold by the mob.

After a trip across the Susquehanna River to Barbara's Endicott plant revealed no suspicious activity, Croswell and Vasisko drove back seven miles to the Barbara's fieldstone mansion on the highest hill in the area. The palatial Barbara mansion sat just off a lightly traveled dirt road with no fences or shielding trees and no guards—if you didn't count the two friendly boxer dogs that roamed the grounds and barked whenever strangers arrived. When Croswell and Vasisko got to the rambling mansion about 7 p.m. on Nov. 13, 1957, they found four high-priced and highly-maintained cars in the driveway. Croswell's check showed one of those cars belonged to Patsy Turrigiano, an Endicott ex-con. One belonged to James LaDuca, Magaddino's son-in-law. Another was registered to a New Jersey man and the fourth was registered to a Cleveland, Ohio company known as Buckeye Cigarette Service.

Because Turrigiano was at the Barbara mansion, Croswell figured it might be a meeting about bootlegging and he contacted Arthur Ruston and Kenneth Brown who worked the area for the U.S. Treasury Department's Alcohol and Tobacco Tax Unit and whom he trusted from past work together. While waiting for the

ATU agents to arrive, Croswell drove back to the motel and asked the owners to see if they could get registration cards signed by any of the men who had arrived about 8:30 p.m. that day and gone directly to one of the rooms Joey B. had booked hours earlier. The motel owners said they were ready to throw the men out because they had refused to sign in as requested, but Croswell got them to keep the men in the room as a favor to the police. He told the husband and wife operating the motel that he and his co-workers "can keep an eye on them here."

At about 11:30 p.m. on Nov. 13, 1957, the car driven by Magaddino's son-in-law LaDuca arrived at the Vestal motel. Croswell and his small team staked out both the Barbara mansion and the motel until early in the morning. What fueled Croswell's interest about the situation in November 1957 had been the October 1956 speeding arrest in nearby Binghamton of reputed mob killer and Brooklyn vending machine company operator Carmine Galante. In the fall of 1956 Galante, also known as Lilo and who later became a ranking Capo and street boss of New York City's powerful Bonanno crime family, spent 30 days in the nearby Broome County jail and was fined $150 after giving a false name. Two years after Galante's arrest, Police Chief Frederick Roos, Captain Chris Gleitmann and Sgt. Peter Policastro of the West New York, New Jersey police force and Ernest J. Mordarelli, director of public safety of that city directly across the Hudson River from New York City, were indicted for official corruption.

On July 12, 1979, some five months after Galante's latest brief imprisonment on parole violation charges, the then 69-year-old mobster was assassinated as he was eating lunch at Joe and Mary's Italian-American Restaurant in the Bushwick section of Brooklyn. The shooting was apparently payback by the Gambino crime family for the murders of Gambino associates during an intense war between the two crime families in the 1970s over control of New York City drug trafficking.

But on Nov. 13, 1957, while monitoring the Barbara estate through the early morning hours, Croswell and Vasisko saw three expensive cars drive in and park outside Barbara Senior's McFall Road home. They also found an Ohio-registered car parked outside the Parkway Motel and belonging to one of the men who had refused to sign the motel register and had told the motel staff that Joey Barbara "will take care of" the bill. Alerting Albany of the situation and calling U.S. Treasury agents Arthur Ruston and Kenneth Brown to come to their Vestal substation, Croswell and Vasisko kept monitoring the arrival of more expensive out-of-area cars until well into the next morning. The legal fireworks started about 12:30 p.m. Nov. 14, 1957 as Croswell and Vasisko and the two Treasury agents drove to the Barbara estate and were spotted by one of Barbara's henchmen as they were taking down the license plate numbers of the nearly three dozen expensive cars parked all over the Barbara property. Knowing that two of the three roads leading out of the Barbara estate were impassible because they were blocked by fallen bridges, the Croswell-led troopers set up a roadblock a mile from the Barbara property on the only accessible road. Over a dozen troopers who had been called in to help ended up assisting in chasing the "suits" who had run into the nearby woods after being alerted to the presence of uniformed officers outside the mansion.

Russell Alberto Bufalino was a Magaddino cousin and the reputed boss of mob operations in northern Pennsylvania and lower New York State. Bufalino kept control of his "family"' operations which included a lucrative, multi-state, multi-million dollar "arson-for-hire" operation even after he ended up in federal prison. Bufalino died on Feb. 25, 1994 of natural causes at the age of 90. In his younger years he worked with Barbara for Magaddino in the Buffalo area. Bufalino has long been suspected of having ordered the "assignment" that resulted in the 1975 assassination of former Teamsters president Jimmy Hoffa by Frank "The Irishman" Sheeran, a longtime friend of both Hoffa and Bufalino. Sheeran said as much in his 2004 book "I Heard You Paint Houses" which hit the stands shortly before his own death. Bufalino, a member of the Teamsters Union himself and a longtime labor racketeer, was never prosecuted for the Hoffa murder. The dying Sheeran claimed Hoffa's body could not be found because it had been cremated immediately after the killing.

The Mother of All Raids

Shortly after the November 1957 raid, Bufalino was quoted as claiming the Barbara estate gathering had only been a "cookout" that drew "visitors from all parts of the country and what's wrong with that?"

It was about 12:30 p.m. on Nov. 14, 1957 when Croswell began taking down the license plate numbers on the nine expensive cars parked in front of the four-car garage on the Barbara estate. As he was taking down the plate numbers, a young Dalmatian pup in the nearby kennel began barking and ten men who had been behind the garage stepped out. Some of them began yelling and some ran back to the house. Croswell found about 25 more expensive Cadillacs, Imperials, and Lincolns parked on the property. He also found a big stone barbecue at the back of the garage covered with sizzling steaks for the picnic lunch that had been planned. And as Croswell drove back down the hill about a mile he told his fellow raiders "Let's find out who Joe's got at his party."

After calling for reinforcements, Croswell and federal agent Ruston remained at the roadblock about a mile down from the Barbara estate. About 1 p.m. a truck driven by Bartolo Guccia stopped at the roadblock, quickly turned around and drove back to the mansion. Moments later Croswell could see various Barbara guests running like frightened deer across the open fields around the mansion into the nearby woods. Just then an expensive new Imperial driven by Russell Bufalino came down to the roadblock. In the Bufalino car were the pasty-faced Vito Genovese, known as the most powerful man in the underworld and boss of the northeastern U. S. and three lesser mob figures.

When Croswell asked the men "what are you fellows doing up here?," Genovese politely said "Do we have to answer your questions?" Knowing he didn't have to say anything, Genovese gave Croswell a crooked smile and the five mobsters got back in the car and drove off. Vito Genovese, then running New York City's biggest Mafia family and a would-be Napoleon then eyeing control of Mafia operations nationwide, was denounced by former New York Governor Thomas E. Dewey as "king of the rackets." Genovese was later convicted of narcotics conspiracy.

The Mother of All Raids

On the 50th anniversary of the historic raid that made "Mafia" a household word, retired New York State Police trooper Frederick Tiffany recalled that after Croswell's team had been spotted writing down the plates, he had been called on to fire a warning shot into the air. Tiffany recalled seeing "scores of men" running from Barbara's house into the nearby wood from all the doors of the palatial abode. Recalling that day from his home in Oswego, New York, 50 years later, Tiffany, then one of the last living Apalachin raiders, said it was "some kind of a clambake" with dozens of men in expensive silk suits suddenly running to some of the parked cars if not dashing into the nearby woods.

Within hours Croswell had seventeen uniformed troopers helping him escort 60 Barbara guests to his tiny trooper station in Vestal.

Only nine of the group proved to be clean and without criminal records. The 51 others had 275 prior arrests and 100 convictions. But none of them were currently on any law enforcement "wanted" lists and none proved to be carrying illegal weapons. Few were carrying personal papers or wallets and aside from their driver's licenses almost all had large rolls of cash, mostly $50s and $100s. Many claimed they had all just managed to stop to see Barbara at the same time, having heard he was sick. "And, of course, they told us this with straight faces, too," Croswell later recalled. However, Croswell discovered that Barbara's staff had placed a $431 order of steak, veal cutlets, ham and canned luncheon meats at a Binghamton store a week before the raid to be rushed from a Chicago packing house. Croswell also found that 19 of Barbara's guests had arrived at the Broome County Airport on Nov. 14 on the same TWA flight from Newark, N. J. All of them had registered for the flight using fake names which he and other investigators confirmed were the names of unsuspecting neighbors of the mobsters.

During the cursory questioning of suspects the day of the raid, reputed mobster Simone Scoizzari of San Gabriel, California, told the Croswell team he had been "unemployed for 20 years," despite having $9,000 in cash on him that day. Croswell let Binghamton Sun reporter David Rossie, later a top Central New York

16

newspaper columnist, who had been regularly making routine police checks at the Vestal barracks, sit in on the interrogations, including Scoizzari's. Years later, Rossie told the Binghamton Press-Bulletin about how so many of those well-dressed men wearing thousand-dollar suits "acted like I was from another planet" since he was, in his own words, "just a raggedy-ass reporter."

Several of Barbara's guests found in the woods near his mansion claimed during their interrogations that they had arrived in the area from New Jersey on the Pennsylvania Railroad just to scout out possible real estate investments. When one of those real estate mavens was told by the Croswell team that the railroad line didn't come within 70 miles or so of Apalachin, he reportedly just shrugged his shoulders and said "I don't know why you fellows don't believe us."

Magaddino's son-in-law James LaDuca was stopped near Binghamton late on the afternoon of Nov. 14, 1957. LaDuca's clothing was disheveled and his shoes dirty and muddy because he and three equally dirty companions had obviously just run through the woods from Barbara's backyard to the Vestal motel to get a car and drive away, but he still claimed he had simply been driving through Binghamton back to Buffalo after a business trip. LaDuca later returned to the Barbara mansion where his father-in-law had remained inside the mansion safe from arrest by the warrantless raiders. LaDuca drove the Real Teflon Don back to Lewiston three days after the raid.

Croswell later scoffed at the claims of Bufalino and Barbara's other guests, including noted Buffalo business and political figure John C. Montana, about why they had all decided, on their own, to stop to visit their ailing friend Barbara. Croswell said "They were dressed just about like Hollywood gangsters—dark coats, wide-brim hats, white-on-white shirts, pointed shoes and dark suits hand-tailored from imported cloth."

It turned out that while there were some younger mobsters present, many of the delegates to Barbara's get-well barbeque were 50 to 65 years old and over 30 were foreign-born but all had no trouble speaking or understanding English—until later in various courtrooms and before investigative government committees when a number of them claimed they had trouble understanding English. Joe "Olive Oil King" Profaci claimed he ended up in Apalachin by mistake after taking a wrong turn while driving from New York City to Scranton, Pa. Profaci claimed that when he realized he was near the home of his old friend Barbara, he decided it would be the perfect opportunity to stop in and see his friend.

Anthony Guarnieri claimed he was in the business of selling men's and women's clothing and just happened to be in Endicott on Nov. 14, 1957 when he ran into Patsy Turrigiano who said he was going over to see Barbara and asked if he'd like to join him. Guarnieri said it was by "amazing coincidence" that he had just made three custom-sized shirts for Barbara which he had been planning to mail to the businessman, so the visit proved ideal.

Bartolo Guccia, the Endicott thug who had been the first to test the Croswell roadblock, claimed he had been at the Barbara residence that day picking up an order of fish, something he claimed he did on a weekly basis. When asked why he had been driving back up to the Barbara mansion after passing the roadblock, Guccia denied having been sent down to check it out and insisted he went back because he had—for some reason—forgotten to put the fish order in his truck. Pressed about what fish he had obtained at the Barbara mansion, Guccio said "three porgies and a mackerel."

John C. Montana, the Buffalo businessman and former elected city official, proved to be one of the crown jewels of the raid. After being helped off a fence where his expensive suit got snared, Montana claimed he had been driving to Pittston, Pa. on business when the Cadillac he bought brand new only two or three months earlier developed brake trouble near the home of his long-time friend Joe Barbara. Though Montana was ultimately one of the 20 defendants convicted of contempt for his claims—only to have all those convictions overturned on appeal —the day of the raid he claimed he was sure Barbara would have a mechanic available who could perform whatever brake repair he needed. He insisted that was the only reason he ended up at the Barbara residence when the Croswell crusaders showed up.

The Mother of All Raids

Not all of the partygoers proved to be as initially cooperative as Montana. John DeMarco of Shaker Heights, a Cleveland suburb, and John Scalish of Cleveland both refused to cooperate. Croswell found DeMarco and Scalish were both veterans of the Ohio State prison system and DeMarco had been linked in the past to murders, blackmail and a mob-related bombing in Ohio and Scalish served time on robbery and parole violation counts. DeMarco and Scalish were paid back by being the last two detainees held at the Vestal station.

Croswell and Lts. K.E. Weidenborner and J.A. Murphy realized that under then-existing New York State criminal law there was no way they could legally detain any of the partygoers on even minor misdemeanor counts since they couldn't prove any of them had been consorting for unlawful purposes. DeMarco and Scalish were the last of the mobsters released from detention about 1:30 a.m. Nov. 15, 1957. "It almost broke our hearts to have to toss all those big ones back," Croswell later said.

Though no one taken for questioning after the raid could be held for prosecution—except for later contempt convictions which were ditched by the higher courts—the Apalachin raid had torn away the veil of secrecy that had protected the Mafia for decades directly under the gaze of J. Edgar Hoover and his FBI. Croswell's team had given law enforcement agencies nationwide an authentic look at the size of the criminal syndicate for the first time, confirming the connections between New York City's Murder Incorporated, Detroit's Purple Gang, the old Capone mob in Chicago and mob activities in California, Cleveland, Florida and New Orleans. The November 1957 raid also led to Barbara being pressured to sell his lucrative bottling plant which had served for over a decade as a convenient front for mob bootlegging operations.

"We convinced Mr. (J. Edgar) Hoover that there was such a thing as organized crime," a gloating Joseph J. Benenati, the former sheriff of Chenango County and one of the last surviving members of the Apalachin raiders, recalled shortly after he celebrated his 93rd birthday at the New York State Veterans Home in Oxford in 2007.

He died on July 28, 2011 at age 97. At the time of the raid, he was Supervisor of BCI's Criminal Intelligence Unit C.

Benenati was one of the state troopers protecting FDR and his family when they would return to their Hyde Park estate and he joined the Marines because FDR's son Jimmy, already a Marine, talked him into it. Benenati, who risked his life on Guam to direct artillery and flame throwers at bunkered Japanese troops finally got the Brown Star that he earned for that action almost 50 years later. In 2007 Benenati recalled with quiet glee that to J. Edgar Hoover the success of the Apalachin Raid "was a kick in the ass." Before earning a battlefield commission in the South Pacific during WWII, Benenati had been one of the State Police's first "Grey Riders" on horseback in the late 1930s. He was a Bureau of Criminal Investigation sergeant when Gov. Rockefeller appointed him sheriff in 1960, a job he held election after election until he retired in 1983.

Benenati recalled that "thousands" of dollars but no handguns or other weaponry were recovered from the mobsters arrested in the woods outside Barbara's sprawling estate. He recalled being surprised to see so many well-dressed men come racing out of Barbara's mansion and heading for the woods. That sight looked just like "flushing a bevy of quail" out into the open air, he said. After Rockefeller made the World War II hero a county sheriff, he said Rocky "used to call me to talk about" the Apalachin raid from time to time "and how we ruined their barbeque."

Still powerfully built at the age of 93, the 6 foot, 4 inch Benenati joked in 2007 about how the mobsters surrendered meekly once caught or found hanging on wire fences or entangled in underbrush in the woods hours after the Barbara barbeque was aborted due to the quickly-planned raid. After Benenati's retirement the Chenango County Sheriff's Department created the Benenati Award in his honor which it presents to officers for career achievements and outstanding performance in the field of law enforcement. A Joe Benenati Day is celebrated annually in that Central New York county as well.

The speed of putting together the raid had prevented Croswell and his associates from obtaining legally-required search warrants from judges to go into the Barbara mansion, a predicament that haunted the gifted policeman until his dying day. Melvin John Blossom, the disabled caretaker of the Barbara estate who became a good friend of Benenati after the raid and Norman Joseph Russell, whose wife was the Barbara family's maid, both later confirmed for Benenati that Magaddino and the other heavy hitters had managed to avoid the humiliation of a public arrest by remaining inside Barbara's mansion with the ailing mobster and his wife and house staff.

At least four of Barbara's overlords, Stefano Magaddino, Tommy "Three Fingers Brown" Lucchese, Carmine Galante and John LaRocca were safely driven from the grounds three days after the raid by Jimmy LaDuca and Barbara's son Joey and Emanuel Zicari an Endicott, New York counterfeiter and laborer at the Endicott-Johnson Shoe Company who in 1959 was a pallbearer at the funeral of Barbara Senior. Blossom and Russell told Benenati the autos of John Montana and Stefano Magaddino's son-in-law Jimmy LaDuca were hidden in the barn on the Barbara estate, also unsearchable due to the lack of search warrants the day of the raid.

Not so lucky the day of the raid were Cuban mob boss Santo Trafficante, a/k/a, Louis Santos who played a large role in the daytime assassination of Anastasia as a message to other wannabes; north Pennsylvania mob chieftain Russell Bufalino; Vito Genovese; Joseph Profaci, a Brooklyn "businessman" and ex-con from his native Italy who was a high-ranking associate of Genovese; Frank Costello, and many others in the mob's upper circle including Carlo Gambino and his brother-in-law Paul Castellano of Brooklyn; Central New York mob boss Salvatore Falcone of Utica and Kansas City, Mo. drug kingpins Nick Civella and Joseph Filardo.

In the woods, John C. Montana, 64, the prominent Buffalo, New York businessman and former Buffalo city councilman who only a year earlier had been publicly lauded by a Buffalo-area law enforcement group and the local news media as that city's "man of the year" for his public and charitable endeavors, was personally found by Croswell hanging from a fence near the Barbara estate in an expensive suit. Montana, the wealthy operator of a Buffalo taxi company and liquor distributorship and a Buffalo taxi company only later identified by law enforcement as a key Magaddino operative, had initially admitted to Croswell's raiders that he had driven to Barbara's that day with Magaddino's brother Antonino "Nino" Magaddino.

But Montana later told the New York State Commission of Investigation that he had actually been on a business trip in Central New York and only drove to the Barbara home the day of the raid looking for a mechanic because he began experiencing car trouble near Oswego. Montana had been one of Magaddino's top confidants from the 1930s and was a powerful Buffalo area Republican politician who made an unsuccessful bid for the U.S. Congress. He told the New York State Investigative commission looking into the Apalachin raid that he had merely had a pleasant round of tea with Mrs. Barbara while waiting for an auto mechanic to come. He never clearly explained why he ran into the woods and tried to scale the fence where his expensive suit got snared. Montana insisted to his dying day that he was surprised to find a big party underway at the Barbara mansion and that he had remained in a separate room apart from the other "guests" while waiting for the repairs on his vehicle. But Croswell told state investigators that when he pulled Montana down from the fence the day of the raid Montana had promised to get him promoted if he would just let him go away quietly.

Also nabbed at the roadblock, in the woods and on nearby highways were Dominic Alaimo of Pittston, Penn, a committeeman for Local 8005 of the United Mine Workers Union and president of Pittston's Jane Hogan Dress Co. Inc; and Joseph "Joey" Mario Barbara Jr., the son of the 'host' who refused to answer any questions when he was stopped driving from the estate in a station wagon owned by his father's Canada Dry Bottling Co. of Endicott, NY.

The day after the raid, Joey was arrested by Endicott police for assaulting a photographer from the New York Journal American who had been sent as part of the team covering the historic event. No record was preserved of the verdict in that assault case and Joey moved to Detroit after the death of his father, hooking up with the Detroit "family." Two years after the Apalachin raid, Joey, a former "sales manager" for his father's bottling company, was charged with five counts of perjury for his testimony before the state commission of investigation.

Other party attendees came from New York City, Brooklyn, various towns in New Jersey—South Orange, Palisades, Atlantic Heights, Highland Park, Linden, Elizabeth, Camden, West Orange; Buffalo, NY, Dallas, Texas, Pueblo, Colorado, Boston, Mass.; Shaker Heights, Ohio; Downey, Calif.; Gibsonia, Penn.; Johnson City, NY; Auburn, NY; East Islip, NY; New Kingston, PA.; Forest Hills, NY; Lido Beach, NY; Yonkers, Jackson Heights, Cleveland, San Gabriel, Calif. Rochester, NY and Sagamon, Illinois.

The only mobster to escape from the raid was Chicago boss Sam Giancana. Giancana ran into the fields and eluded the troopers. He ended up at a food market and is believed to have hitched a ride out of town.

Croswell never overcame his anger at being rebuked by various appellate judges who castigated him for hauling the Barbara "visitors" in for questioning on that rainy day in November 1957.

Joe "The Barber" Barbara Sr. who had been leery about Magaddino's plan for the summit because of police problems following the mob meeting at his estate a year earlier, died of a heart attack on June 17, 1959. Barbara, the once powerful mob grandee of New York's Tioga County and a former Magaddino crime family worker in Buffalo decades earlier, went to his grave forever immortalized in prosecution court papers as the "host" of the Apalachin Meeting.

Joe Valachi, the federal government's top mobster-turned-informant, described the Apalachin meeting to Congress as an attempt by Magaddino and the other bosses to split up the New York crime network of Albert "The Mad Hatter" Anastasia, a former Murder Inc. executioner who had been assassinated by two masked men during a daylight incident in the barber shop of Manhattan's Park Sheraton Hotel on Oct. 25, 1957 under orders of Genovese. Valachi told congressmen the meeting was also set to reorganize the command structure of New York City area rackets in coin-operated slot machines, pinball machines, vending and washing machines and to reorganize the mob-controlled New York

City garbage-hauling industry and "buy off" as many judges and politicians throughout the country as possible.

Anastasia, who had killed his way into the top rungs of the mob's operations in New York City and beyond, was gunned down because of his reputed lust for the lucrative Havana, Cuba casino operations of mob financier Meyer Lansky and Tampa, Florida-based Santo Trafficante Jr., according to Valachi and others.

On Sept. 29, 1958—some nine months before Joe "The Barber" Barbara died of his chronic heart problems, BCI Sgt. Benenati went to the Barbara estate to try to serve a subpoena on Barbara on behalf of the State Commission of Investigation which had begun public hearings on the raid on August 12, 1958. Mrs. Barbara answered the doorbell but she refused to open it, claiming her husband was sick and she refused to disturb him. Benenati called the Barbaras the next day only to have the impending widow tell him her husband was unable to come to the phone and physically unable to accept service of the subpoena.

That prompted the veteran lawman to return to the Barbara mansion and begin circling the house ringing bells and knocking on doors—all with no response—until he saw the Barber lying in bed in a first floor bedroom. After Benenati began tapping on the window and calling out to Barbara in a loud voice, Mrs. Barbara came and pulled the window curtains shut. Benenati got Mrs. Barbara to come to the front door but peeking through curtains she told the lawman she would not let him into her house. Though Benenati left the subpoena and what he later described as the "appropriate witness fee" for Barbara's testimony before the Commission, Mrs. Barbara yelled out to him that she would not touch the subpoena and that it had not been served, apparently more conversant in the law than most Central New York housewives. With that, Benenati, who had survived withering Japanese gunfire on Guam over a decade earlier, began walking around the outside of the Barbara mansion with a portable amplifier restating why he was there. The old sarge spoke in a voice loud enough that another state trooper parked a fifth of a mile from the house later told superiors he could clearly hear what Benenati was telling the dying mobster.

The Mother of All Raids

Within a few months, the Croswell-led raid began to have an impact on law enforcement efforts against organized crime. In the spring of 1958 the U.S. Justice Department finally announced its plans to either imprison or deport "100 Top Hoodlums" through a joint effort of the FBI, the federal Immigration Service, the IRS, the Federal Bureau of Narcotics and the U.S. Treasury Department. The National Association of State Attorneys General and several other state government organizations pledged to aid that federal effort and the Justice Department created a Special Group on Organized Crime.

Russell Bufalino and Joe Profaci were the first of the mob big-wigs ordered deported and Genovese and three of the other Apalachin party goers were convicted of importing and selling narcotics.

Though many theories were passed around law enforcement about the true reason for the November 1957 barbeque at the Barbara mansion, Croswell was sure nothing was accomplished by 'the boys" during their aborted "summit." "From what we know of their activities we're inclined to believe that they had very little time to discuss anything before the party was broken up," Croswell said months after the raid. "Most of them had just arrived on the morning of November 14th and the early part of the program seemed to be devoted to eating and drinking and renewing old acquaintances," he said. "Then we arrived on the scene." Croswell also stressed that motel and hotel reservations for the partygoers showed virtually all had been slated to spend at least two nights there. "Undoubtedly they planned to do a lot of business but I guess we spoiled that," Croswell added.

Croswell was publicly lauded by a number of professional law enforcement groups for the seminal work he did in 1957 in exposing La Cosa Nostra, including being named Man of the Year in 1958 by the Society of Professional Investigators. But Croswell was largely given the cold shoulder by his State Police superiors, with no promotion, salary increase or citations on his departmental record for his herculean effort at Apalachin.

Some of that departmental animosity was probably caused by Croswell's arrest, shortly after the raid, of a New York City newspaper reporter who stole some confidential documents from Croswell's desk when Croswell was called from his Vestal office on assignment. After a friend of Croswell's at the Endicott, New York newspaper called him and said the reporter had photocopied the documents at the news office, Croswell arrested him when he tried to sneak the documents back into Crowell's files. Though Croswell just took the documents back from the reporter and sent him on his way without taking him to court, the reporter's paper quickly had a Page One story falsely blasting Croswell for allegedly botching a chance to keep a lot of the crime lords picked up in the raid behind bars. When that newspaper demanded official investigations of Croswell, both the Governor and State Police officials launched them, only to have Croswell come through with flying colors.

In the final report on the raid by the New York Joint Legislative Committee on Government Operations, Croswell was lauded publicly for what the legislative committee cited as his "superior" work. The legislative panel noted the "insufficient legal basis"—because of procedural short comings in state criminal law—for holding the mobsters after they had been interrogated. In its final report that legislative committee stressed that without Croswell's efforts the Apalachin mob convention likely would have passed unnoticed and at best in the future become "no more than another rumor in law enforcement circles" about mob activities.

Now one of the legends of New York State and national law enforcement, Croswell later became chief investigator for State Police vice operations in Utica, retiring in 1966 as a captain and getting a job as inspector general of the New York City Department of Sanitation. From 1970 until his second law enforcement retirement in 1979, Croswell was an investigator for the New York State Organized Crime Task Force, one of the many law enforcement operations that owe their existence to his groundbreaking work on Nov. 14, 1957. With the help of the Forest Avenue Boys own crack Sicilian-language translator Tony Dirienz, he broke the back of a major Europe-to-New York drug smuggling ring in the 1970s.

Croswell died in November 1990 at the age of 77 with little public fanfare. Today the FBI openly lauds him for what it describes as his "important detective work" in exposing a veritable Who's Who of organized crime and uncovering a conspiratorial web of racketeers across the country with its activities extending into Puerto Rico and pre-Castro Cuba.

Hoover's Top Hoodlum Program, which he launched after Croswell's seminal work on that Tioga County hillside in 1957, produced a wealth of information about organized crime activities and prompted the Congress to toughen federal laws dealing with mob-controlled gambling and enact new laws that unlocked the mob's financial networks, including the Omnibus Crime Control Act of 1968 and the Racketeer Influenced and Corrupt Organizations Act of 1970.

* * * * *

What was the real reason for the Apalachin summit? This was disclosed to Trooper Benenati sometime later by Melvin Blossom, the estate's caretaker whom Benenati had befriended. The Mob wanted to extend its control over American business and politics through nefarious means such as uncovering the dirty little secrets of powerful men in politics and business and using that information to extort their way into their fiefdoms. That's why John Montana, Magaddino's political and business liaison, was at the meeting. The dream was less about carving up existing territory than about greatly expanding the empire itself. That dream was interrupted when Montana was caught hanging off a fence trying to escape from the troopers.

2.   The Office

The majestic twin teal-topped Richardson Towers graced the old New York State Asylum for the Insane in Buffalo, New York. The facility was designed by Henry Hobson Richardson in the 19th Century to complement the landscaping of Frederick Law Olmsted, the founder of landscape architecture, champion of the City Beautiful movement in the latter half of that century and designer of Buffalo's lovely park system and the Central Park of another New York State metropolis. The working farm on the northern portion of the Asylum grounds provided both work and food for its patients and later became the campus of Buffalo State College. The Richardson Towers complex entered the 21st Century as part of the renamed Buffalo Psychiatric Center and the renamed Richardson-Olmsted complex stands as a graceful reminder of the Queen City's 19th Century elegance.

For almost a decade in the mid-20th Century, a highly-motivated team of New York State Police investigators labored away in an abandoned laundry in Building No. 25—behind the Towers on the asylum grounds at Forest and Elmwood avenues, telephonically boring their way, 24 hours a day, seven days a week into the belly of the beast that was Stefano Magaddino's "Arm," his long-thriving criminal empire.

Before succumbing to the political witch hunts that crimped many law enforcement operations nationwide in the early 1970s, the Forest Avenue Boys' efforts produced numerous successful State Police operations, alone and with other law enforcement agencies, against Magaddino's Niagara Falls-based operations whose criminal tentacles spread north to Toronto, west to Cleveland, south

29

through northwestern Pennsylvania and east into Utica in Central New York.

Because of the clandestine nature of its work, the secret unit operating behind Richardson's 18th century masterworks was never publicly credited or even mentioned by its State Police commanders and remained unknown to the Western New York news media and Magaddino's Arm. The Boys' production was in sharp contrast to the ultimate failure of FBI efforts to put Magaddino behind bars.

Richardson Towers

The Forest Avenue Boys ("the Boys"), formally known as the Buffalo Special Investigations Unit of the New York State Police, achieved victory after victory over Magaddino's mob after it moved out of a typically nondescript New York State Police office in the basement of Troop A's Athol Springs Station south of Buffalo. Though the Boys operated together clandestinely for less than a decade, its infiltration into the guts of the Magaddino crime family provided law enforcement officials nationwide with a look at the internal workings of the Mob and how its criminal tactics were worked out and implemented.

While the FBI never publicly recognized the accomplishments of the Forest Avenue Boys, FBI officials adopted and utilized many of the techniques the secret team developed to get listening devices into the cars, homes and businesses of mobsters. The work of the

The Office

Forest Avenue Boys also gave law enforcement nationwide an insight into the thinking of the Magaddino family's chief operatives, something that proved tactically fruitful against mobsters nationwide in later decades. In addition to the intelligence gathered by the Forest Avenue Boys, a number of crimes planned by Magaddino's minions were either halted or foiled with quick arrests.

On dozens of occasions, the Boys had to hold off on alerting Henry F. Williams, head of the State Police Batavia-based Troop A and the Boys' liaison, and their other superiors about specific mob operational plans. Their concern was that a law enforcement raid or seizure linked to their operation would alert Magaddino's boys to the fact that dozens of their homes and telephones and Buffalo-area restaurants where they met to discuss their "business" plans were bugged. Magaddino would have altered communication routes if the Boys' work was uncovered because he ran his crime family with army-like precision until the ravages of old age took their toll in the late 1960s and early 1970s.

Though it bothered the Forest Avenue Boys to see the commission of crimes they had some advance knowledge of, their concerns were routinely relieved listening to all the outraged telephone calls between Magaddino's operatives complaining and pointing accusatory fingers at each other—in both profane English and Sicilian—when a mob operation had been thwarted through their secret work.

New York State Police planners involved in a governor-backed launch in the early 1960s of secret teams like the Forest Avenue Boys to electronically dig into the same corners of the crime empires of Magaddino and other Mafia barons wrongly anticipated minimum accomplishments at best. What developed though was much better than the disastrous and heavy-handed FBI efforts that did not garner much useful information. One of Magaddino's operatives likely discovered the FBI bugs and made sure crime planning and even references to the names of Magaddino's "generals" and higher ups were never referred to in any of the FBI-bugged locations.

Once the Forest Avenue Boys went to work, they quickly found Magaddino's troops operated like a highly-disciplined military force, which in a criminal way they were. For example, after picking up intelligence about Santasiero's Restaurant, the Boys bugged the place at 1329 Niagara Street at Lafayette Avenue in mid-summer 1965. They confirmed through that tap that "Sam" Pieri and Joe DiCarlo and others used it as their operational headquarters, joining forces there from about noon to 3:30 p.m. each day of the week. "Sam" Pieri proved routinely abrasive in talks picked up on the Santasiero's phone tap and live wire in the restaurant's back room where Pieri and his associates frequently met to discuss mob business.

It soon became clear that when the Real Teflon Don himself, Magaddino, would come to Santasiero's with at least two armed guards, all his men would kiss his right hand to show their respect. From the Santasiero's wiretap, the Boys learned that every fall the Real Teflon Don and about 50 of his top guns would meet and discuss "business" seated around four long tables in the back room of Andy's Cafe on Buffalo's Lower Terrace. One of Andy's workers later told investigative reporter Lee Coppola that Magaddino was never "loud or boisterous like a lot of others" in attendance at those annual sessions. Magaddino "was like Santa Claus," the Coppola source continued, "He smiled with his eyes."

In the fall of 1964 the Boys also bugged a public telephone outside Buffalo's legendary Town Casino. Magaddino's Buffalo big wigs, including Freddy Randaccio, frequented that famed night club and used that "safe" public telephone for mob business calls. The Boys also put a tap on a similar public telephone outside Buffalo's famed 31 Club at Elmwood Avenue and Johnson Park where Buffalo Mayor Sedita and his government, business and close associates frequently dined. Magaddino's upper echelon also frequented that establishment.

The wiretaps on the homes of Johnny Sacco on Buffalo's Bedford Avenue and Inwood Place confirmed that Magaddino soldiers burned down an office building at Elmwood and Utica Avenues in 1965 to cover their theft of thousands of dollars worth of American Express checks that Sacco planned to sell to his New York City mob associates. They used a 12-year-old boy to plant a timed fire-bomb to set the fire. Unit Co-Commander Maury Gavin alerted U.S. Postal Services investigators who took over that investigation. The Sacco wires also led to the breakup of a

The Office

Magaddino-controlled auto theft ring in the late 1960s that, with assistance from several Buffalo area junkyards, generated six-figure profits for the Arm.

The Forest Avenue Locus

When George Karalus got assigned to the unit from Troop A in 1964, all it had in its small Athol Springs basement operations room were three wiretaps of illegal gambling operations in Buffalo and Niagara Falls. In the summer of 1964 word came down from Troop A that the wiretap operation had to be relocated to a secure office far away from any obvious Trooper operational units and off the police agency's operational charts. In August 1964 Maury Gavin had equipment removed from the Athol Springs basement and driven to the New York State Psychiatric Hospital grounds at Forest Avenue and Elmwood Avenue, a part of the city's West Side known to be a breeding ground and home to many of the Magaddino Arm's soldiers and commanders.

Gavin took the men through the mental hospital grounds at 400 Forest, joking with them about the thought of camping out in the mob's home territory and in the midst of so many psychiatrically-troubled individuals. At the back of the hospital grounds Gavin stopped at a broken down two-story brick building designed by Richardson that had once functioned as the hospital's laundry but which was long abandoned like several nearby buildings and which were torn down after the mid-1970s. Though the old laundry building proved to be the home to a bunch of rats of the non-human kind, it was deemed by Gavin and Frenchy Rivard, the unit co-commander, to be the ideal location for the secret headquarters.

The old laundry building was a regular dust bin and mental patients allowed to leave their rooms would constantly be walking around the building on their daytime constitutionals. The abandoned building was close to the side street known as Reese Street and adjacent to Grant Street, a major city thoroughfare. And with additional entrances to the hospital grounds off Elmwood and Forest avenues, it provided lots of space for the unit's cars to park unnoticed. The location of the building housing the unit's operations was so inconspicuous that it allowed the team members to slip in and out simply by driving down Reese which runs parallel to Grant. The mental hospital operation was officially described in State Police files as a facility for "storage and training" of troopers. Despite the remoteness of the building on the mental hospital grounds, Gavin and Rivard were constantly afraid the operation would be publicly exposed. They both harped to their cohorts to be careful entering the hospital grounds without calling attention to themselves.

Unit Headquarters—The Old Laundry Building

The first and second floors of the old hospital laundry building, spanning 75 feet by 40 feet, were replete with broken windows and dirt, grime and odor. It took two days to clean up the second floor. The ground floor was left in its unkempt state deliberately. No repairs were done on the outside of the building to maintain the appearance of an abandoned building. Since there were no desks or chairs or other equipment in the large vacant second floor, all that furniture and eavesdropping equipment had to be brought from Athol Springs or borrowed from other state police offices in the Buffalo area. The second floor, which would be the unit's operations center, was provided a new lock for which only team members were given keys. The second floor lavatory and sink were made spotless and a small refrigerator and coffee-making equipment were brought in and an area was set aside for hanging clothes. Two cots were set up for accommodating the night shift.

Gavin, Rivard and Ed Pawlak shared a laugh early on about the special unit being a "next door neighbor" living right in the heart of one of La Cosa Nostra's main areas of operations in Western New York, the West Side of Buffalo.

The Office

After the FBI began making regular visits to the facility, a sound-proof room was built into a corner of the second-floor operation with a desk in the middle of that room for the twenty-four hour, seven day a week monitoring of mob phone calls. Each conversation had to be written down by hand on the yellow legal pads the team shared in the sound-proof room. That inner sound-proof room was the farthest from the stairs to the second floor and behind the office the Boys had set up to keep the operational records of the unit under lock and key.

The Boys much-justified suspicions about the FBI and their mistrust of FBI agents played a major role in the design of the Boys home-away-from-home. They set it up to protect the unit from interlopers—including the FBI!

By late August 1964 the secret room—which became the second home of every member of the team—was fully operational with its wiretapping devices installed as far away as Magaddino's funeral home and home in Niagara Falls and Lewiston thanks to the ineffective wires the FBI dumped on them.

The only person not in the State Police kept up to date about the operations in the unit was Maury Gavin's friend from the New York Telephone Company known as "Red." To ensure security the stairs of the building were rigged so the unit could not be surprised. No mail was ever sent to unit members at the secret site and no visitors from Troop A were ever given guided tours of the site. Trooper George Fitzgerald, skilled in the art of wiretapping, would periodically come from Albany to assist the Boys with installations of wiretaps and live bugs. Under a special deal with a New York Telephone installer known to most of the Boys only as "Red," when an identified mobster's home telephone line was selected as a target, "Red" would alter the phone company's "trouble on the line" connections so that calls from that home or business would automatically go to the Boys instead of to the phone company. In response to "trouble on the line" calls, the Boys would then send out its own "team" of telephone company "repairmen" to "fix" the problem, installing bugging equipment that funneled all calls to and from that telephone line to the Boys' Forest Avenue office.

The Office

It Wasn't Free

The secret operation was costly. To finance its operation, BCI employee Gino D'Angelo maintained accounts for it under the cover of the State Tire Fund to purchase equipment and provide "working" funds the Boys kept on hand to pay for gas purchases and to pay telephone company workers who aided the Boys in their installations and operations and private citizens who assisted the team with information.

D'Angelo purchased a New York Telephone truck the company put up for sale using the "Tire Fund" and listed a non-existent company on the title. D'Angelo was one of the first two accountants hired after State Police Superintendant Arthur Cornelius, a former FBI agent appointed by Gov. Rockefeller to head the state police agency, decided to set up the Special Investigations Unit initially to assist other troop units in major crime investigations. D'Angelo, in a Valentine's Day 2011 interview, told the author the Apalachin raid of 1957 drastically changed the tone and duties of the SIU units. He said his accountant's role with the State Police led to him helping the Forest Avenue Boys get equipment for their job, including the first of the "telephone company" repair trucks they used to alter the Magaddino family's telephone lines. In the 1960s Chrysler had a contract with New York State to supply the government with vans and D'Angelo said he "just cut a purchase order" to get a van for the Boys. But it took Troopers Gavin and George Fitzgerald and their telephone company "connections" to get the phone company 'to agree to let Dodge paint our truck phone company colors."

The Boys kept the truck in Albany and drove it to Western New York as needed. A second New York Telephone truck that the Boys "borrowed" was abandoned after the team was shut down. Captain Bob Cryan, the former FBI agent delegated by Superintendent Cornelius to oversee all the SIU operations, kept a special bank account in his own name to provide funds for the team. The abandoned laundry building at the state hospital site on Forest Avenue came free of charge to the state police.

The Office

Erie County (Buffalo) District Attorney Michael F. Dillon periodically kicked in some funds out of his own budget to show the team and Hank Williams his gratitude for Williams' decision to make sure his old drinking pal Dillon was supplied with all the team's intelligence. Every Friday evening Karalus and later other team members, on orders of unit commander Rivard, would drive to the rear of Buffalo's Meyer Memorial Hospital and turn over to the ever-grateful Dillon a copy of the Boys' weekly reports, the same reports turned over to Williams and Albany trooper heads. Giving the reports to Dillon, one of the state's top prosecutors and later a state appellate judge, proved to be one of Williams' many wise decisions.

Assignments, Not Hits

Soon after the Forest Avenue operation went live, the Boys learned that crossing the Real Teflon Don could and did lead to sudden death for several of his less calculating minions. The Boys, like American movie lovers for decades, were surprised to learn through all the Magaddino-related wires and bugs that Mob-ordered murders were not called "hits" and "contracts" put out by mob bosses on the lives of those marked for death. Rather than those Hollywood-style, Mario Puzo-style assassination words, Magaddino's boys spoke of "assignments" put out after one of Magaddino's key operatives or the Don himself gave the word.

A born killer who grew to appreciate his Western New York aides who also showed a real love for such unofficial "capital punishment," Magaddino would always give the go-ahead for an assignment by raising his hand above his head, the Boys learned. In one of the many sobering moments for the Forest Avenue Boys soon after the secret office went into operation, it became eminently clear that when Magaddino and his henchmen wanted to send a "message" to rivals or rebellious underlings they would have Magaddino or his higher ups dole out an "assignment" to kill the enemy or the mouthy underling.

When the notoriously blood-thirsty Magaddino or one of his top aides wanted the "message" about such persons to be widely advertised, they would make sure the corpse was easily "found" by the authorities and the public and the news media. A case in point was the June 1965 discovery at the intersection of Buffalo's Niagara and Tonawanda streets of a dead man with the rope used to strangle him still wrapped tightly around his neck. When the Real Teflon Don and his crew merely wanted someone eliminated for being ungrateful or unruly, they would be "deposited" near the Niagara Falls Power Plant or laid to rest in the underbelly of one of the coffins containing the earthly remains of someone buried through the Magaddino Niagara Falls funeral parlor.

Lawmen who routinely spied on the Magaddino funeral parlor wondered why even burly pallbearers seemed to have much more difficulty carrying some coffins than others. The Forest Avenue Boys would periodically pick up messages between Magaddino's upper crust confirming that so-and-so was now resting in peace under this or that deceased's remains.

$$$-R-Them

According to wire service reports in early 1971, federal and state law enforcement officials calculated the Mafia's annual take on drug trafficking, gambling and loan sharking to be the equivalent of more than $1 billion of untaxed revenue.

In April 1967, based on the Boys' wiretaps, "Sam" Pieri, brother-in-law of Joe DiCarlo, Buffalo's former Public Enemy No. I, and Salvatore Agro, also of Buffalo, were arrested in the central New York City of Utica by the New York State Police with $20,000 in stolen securities seized in their vehicle. Their car was stopped by a trooper after Agro was spotted changing lanes on the New York State Thruway without signaling. Agro was also charged with trying to bribe the trooper with what turned out to be a $4.75 watch. Agro and Pieri, who had never regained his power in the Magaddino Arm after he returned to Buffalo following a 10-year federal prison term for narcotics trafficking in the early 1950s, were also linked to burglaries in the State of Ohio.

In June 1967, based on information supplied by the Forest Avenue Boys, Freddy Randaccio, Pieri and six others were arrested in Buffalo by federal and state lawmen on a federal indictment linked to a series of holdups nationwide. These included an

The Office

October 1963 robbery of the Fillmore-Glenwood branch of the Marine Midland Trust Co. in Buffalo and a plot to rob an armored car in Los Angeles in early 1965.

In December 1968 as a result of the Forest Avenue Boys' wires, Magaddino, then still widely regarded as the "lord paramount" of mob activities in the western section of New York State and lower Ontario, Canada, was arrested along with his son and eight others, on a federal indictment linked to an alleged Mafia-controlled conspiracy and racketeering operation. Others arrested included two of his main gambling operatives, Benjamin Nicoletti, Sr., then 56, of Lewiston, and his son, Benjamin Jr., then 29, of Niagara Falls.

Also in December 1968, thanks to the Boys' wires, Buffalo police arrested Nicholas A. "Sonny" Mauro, 38, on a North Buffalo street corner as he was carrying over $5,000 in cash and numerous betting records, some stuffed in his socks. Mauro was described at that time as one of Buffalo's biggest bookmakers with an estimated sixty men working under him.

In August 1969, also based on the Boys' wiretaps, Benjamin Nicoletti Jr., then 30, and 18 others were arrested by the FBI and New York State Police for their alleged links to what lawmen described as a $20 million-a-year betting syndicate stretching through Western New York and into lower Ontario, Canada. Nicoletti had to be lowered from the rooftop of a Niagara Falls home in the bucket of a Niagara Falls fire department snorkel during a raid after he fled police entering the building. State Police Investigator Patrick Petrie told the news media Nicoletti had been asked to come down off the roof "but he said he was scared of falling, so we had to send for the snorkel." Neil J. Welch, in 1969 special agent-in-charge of the FBI's Western New York operations, identified Nicoletti Jr. as one of the "key people" in that gambling ring.

In November 1969, also thanks to the Boys' wiretaps, the FBI announced that it had "crippled" a "multimillion dollar" Western New York loan sharking operation run by Albert M. "Babe" Billitteri, a key Magaddino operative. Special Agent Welch and U.S. Attorney H. Kenneth Schroeder told the media the Billiteri operation had been preying on customers ranging from low-paid factory workers and honest businessmen and even bookmakers. Welch also said that such shylocking operations on a national level were a Mafia money maker second only to gambling, with an estimated national take for the mob on loan sharking of about $10 billion.

In December 1969, again thanks to the Boys' wiretaps, Joseph "Spin" Fino, then Magaddino's underboss, and known Cosa Nostra associates Roy Carlisi, Sr. and Salvatore Bonito were subpoenaed to testify before an Erie County grand jury looking into illegal gambling operations in the Buffalo area. All three invoked their Fifth Amendment rights and refused to answer prosecutors' questions.

The Boys' long-running wiretaps on the various phones of Nicholas "Sonny" Mauro, then 40, in March 1970 led to an FBI-led assault on a Mauro-run syndicate gambling operation said to be generating an estimated $9 million to $12 million a year for the Mafia. Its operation was headquartered in a Cherry Street warehouse in Buffalo and was handling bets at the rate of $30,000 to $40,000 a day, six days a week, according to Special Agent Welch. Welch told the news media Mauro was then "Buffalo's top gambler" and was known to refer to himself as "a bookmaker's bookmaker."

In May 1970, again thanks to the Boys' wiretaps, Daniel G. "Boots" Sansanese Sr., then 61, a long-time Magaddino muscle man and gambling overseer, and six other men were charged with running a multi-million-dollar Western New York loansharking operation. Sam Pieri and Sansanese had been running a major loansharking operation with Magaddino's blessing. Sam Rizzo, who served as muscle for the operation would go to Pieri's home with money collected from the debtors. Sansanese was an enforcer as well. One day at Buffalo's Front Park, he grabbed a debtor's hand and tore his thumb off. The man was taken to a Mob-friendly doctor at a local hospital who could be counted on not to report the matter to the police.

In the summer of 1970, the Boys picked up word about a fund-raising stag being planned to help Salvatore Pieri, then 69, pay his legal expenses with the stag to be staged at Painters District Council No. 4 Hall at Elmwood and Virginia in Buffalo. That led to the arrest of Frank Silvestro, then 45, of Guelph, Ontario. Silvestro, a well-known Canadian underworld figure, was arrested by agents of the U.S. Immigration and Naturalization Service after he left the stag which was attended by over 350 persons. "Spin" Fino Sr. and former Buffalo "Public Enemy Nov. 1" Joseph J. DiCarlo, then 70, and Sansanese were reportedly among the crowd at that Pieri fundraiser.

Though the Boys had closed shop months earlier, in November 1972 an Erie County, NY grand jury—thanks to their wiretaps—broke up another Buffalo-based mob-run loansharking operation known to have been charging illegal interest amounts on loans, a violation of New York State's Usury Law.

It was understood on pain of death that Magaddino received thirty percent of the profits of any illegal operation under his jurisdiction, such as gambling and loansharking.

Thanks from Rocky

In mid-September 1964, in the midst of the heated Republican battle over the party's presidential nomination that year, the Boys heard a curious call to "Sam" Pieri from a guy calling from Detroit and asking about a Pieri relative now serving a life term in Ohio on a murder conviction. It seems that Pieri and the guy, later confirmed to be associated with Detroit's notorious Purple Gang, were charting their plan to get Ohio Gov. James A. Rhodes to pardon the Pieri relative who was a key player the Purple Gang wanted back. Rhodes was Ohio's governor from 1963 to 1971 and again from 1975 to 1983 and a top competitor in the GOP 1964 presidential race. The Boys wrote down the discussions between Pieri and his Detroit caller about how a key aide of Rhodes was a homosexual and how the governor could be convinced to release the Pieri relative to spare his top assistant public humiliation at a time when the gay lifestyle was not socially or politically acceptable in polite company.

With New York Governor Rockefeller on the second of his three unsuccessful bids for the GOP presidential nod, the Boys had their tape of the calls about the Pieri relative and the Ohio homosexual and their written transcripts flown to Albany by one of their Mohawk Airline pilot friends who delivered that material directly to Rockefeller's personal secretary. Days later Rocky flew to Columbus, Ohio, for a lunch with Rhodes. Within 24 hours of that lunch in the Ohio state capital, Rhodes publicly announced he was withdrawing his name from consideration for the presidential nomination and throwing his support to Rockefeller. The details of the luncheon never became public knowledge but shortly after the Rhodes' withdrawal from the 1964 presidential race Rocky personally telephoned "Frenchy" Rivard and told him he was "very happy" with all the good work being performed by the Boys.

Albany Bound

Every Friday either Rivard or Pawlak typed out a memo on that week's "harvest" and the memos containing the full transcripts of the calls and tape reels were either flown or driven to Albany to be turned over to State Police supervisory officials for strategy reviews. That material was only driven to Albany if neither of two "friendly and trusted" pilots for the then-operational Mohawk Airline was available to personally deliver them to State Police officials.

The Boys made sure there was corroborating evidence to support all the material they were delivering to higher ups in Albany and to Hank Williams. Every time the wires and bugs produced talk of mob actions that were on the verge of being carried out, that information was rushed to Albany and Hank Williams in Batavia. That was done so higher ups, including Williams, could decide if other State Police units needed to be called into action to deal with the specific mob threat the Boys had uncovered.

In real emergency situations Rivard would use a secure telephone line to alert Albany and Williams as quickly as possible after a talk was monitored. All those procedures were followed with military precision until the unit was shut down permanently.

All the information obtained from the secret wiretaps was religiously passed on to Williams, because he was the superior who routinely arranged for another unit to carry out a raid to ensure that the Forest Avenue unit remained unknown. That anonymity was maintained for eight years until its untimely and ill-advised shutdown in 1972.

Keeping it Legal

After taking over the FBI Magaddino wires, Gavin began asking the G-men about their court-approved monitoring and he kept getting told by FBI "spokesmen" that the court documents had been misplaced but were coming. Those "documents" never surfaced. After the FBI in the late 1960's turned over to the State Police its secret bugs on the home and businesses of Magaddino in the Niagara Falls, N. Y. area, the Forest Avenue Boys were shocked to learn the FBI had never seemed to get court permission for their operations.

The Forest Avenue Boys, in sharp contrast, played by the book and got the required *ex parte* court orders. Magaddino and his Arm and their high-paid attorneys never learned of the operations of the Boys and didn't, despite repeated legal and illegal efforts, track down the leaks that—based on the Boys' intelligence efforts—Hank Williams and his Troop A forces used to foil planned mob heists, recover stolen goods and block plans for assaults on specific targets of the Western New York Mafia. On the other hand, State Police's review of the FBI's wire in Magaddino's home revealed nothing incriminating. This suggested to Gavin and the others on the state police unit that Magaddino had somehow learned of the secret federal government eavesdropping efforts and just refrained from discussing his real "business" within hearing distance of suspected federal listening devices.

The Alleged Kidnapping

On a warm summer's day in 1966 the Boys, under Gavin's command, after confirming that many of Magaddino's Buffalo higher ups including Joe Todaro, Sr., Pieri, Fino and others met regularly at an inconspicuous little luncheonette at the corner of Rhode Island Street and Richmond Avenue near a Buffalo Fire Department station, "kidnapped" a 40-year-old Italian immigrant whose English was still pretty bad after years in the United States.

43

The Office

That happened after they confirmed he lived in a flat directly above the rear table in the luncheonette where the Magaddino forces would discuss "things" over coffee. Maury and Bidwell took the rather flustered immigrant to St. Gerard's Roman Catholic Church at Bailey and East Delavan avenues where an early evening novena service was getting underway.

Outside the church Gavin and Bidwell told the immigrant to go in and pray because they had learned he had done some bad things and they were debating whether to report him to the U.S. Immigration Service and have him deported back to Italy. Bidwell also forcefully told him that if he didn't "become a better citizen" immediately, he would be thrown back on a boat to the old country. The man, who spoke broken English, raised his hands and with a look of abject fear on his face kept shaking his head as he went into the church to pray, hours later walking back to his flat.

Several days later, the Boys went back and took the immigrant back to the church telling him he needed more prayers. His religiosity and the fact that he had to walk back to his flat gave the Boys ample time to secretly plant a "spike mike" in the immigrant's flat right above the table in the ground-floor luncheonette where Magaddino's men were known to sit and talk over their "business." The Boys had confirmed that the luncheonette closed daily between 4 p.m. and 5 p.m. The day of the plant, Karalus stayed outside armed with a Buffalo Police radio to monitor for area patrols, while Gavin and Trooper George Fitzgerald, the skilled State police wire expert from Albany, entered the immigrant's apartment that evening. Gavin just had to lightly jimmy the apartment door open to get inside the flat, so poorly constructed was the building. Moving the bed and a rug, Gavin and Fitz drilled a hole through the wood floor and inserted the "spike mike" directly over the rear table where Magaddino's men always sat, covering it with the rug they had pulled away to get at the flooring. They patched up the apartment floor, pushed back the rug and bed to cover the wire and left.

To the horror of Gavin, when he looked into the front window of the luncheonette he could see sawdust all over the targeted rear table. Breaking open the front door of the joint, the Boys cleaned up the sawdust and tipped over a cash register and some chairs and left the front door closed but unlocked to leave the impression that some hoodlum boys from the neighborhood—a not uncommon occurrence in that neighborhood in the 1960s—had broken into the place looking for money and booze. The immigrant who would have quickly alerted Magaddino's troops, never learned of the hidden mike in his bedroom that proved to be golden for a number of months.

That operation allowed the Boys to pass on valuable tips to Hank Williams so he could arrange to have various units of State Police Troop A headquartered in Batavia either make it known to Magaddino's Arm that they would be closely watching a mob-targeted business or make arrests during a heist that Magaddino's troops had meticulously planned. The Boys also used that "spike mike" to get information they passed on to the Pennsylvania State Police about a mob theft of about 100,000 golf balls and a separate mob theft of a high-priced shipment of beauty supplies. The Boys knew those stolen shipments would be trucked through Ohio but they never trusted Ohio law enforcement. Instead, they passed on their info about the shipments to the Pennsylvania authorities who, next to the Canadian Mounties, were their most trusted law enforcement allies.   After some months of successful operation, that "spike mike" seemed to stop functioning. The Boys did not pick up any chatter on their other wires about Magaddino's troops uncovering that device and just assumed it had malfunctioned. Busy with other wires by then they never tried to re-energize that wire.

Late in the summer of 1966, Maury Gavin opted to set up a live wire in the home of "Joe P.," a notorious stolen property handler who lived in an apartment building on Lafayette Avenue near Gates Circle and Millard Fillmore Hospital. Among the many ironies that struck the Boys about their assignment was that "Joe P" lived only several long blocks away from Justice Mahoney on Lafayette Avenue. Of course the Boys had Mahoney sign the ex parte order for "Joe P's" flat. After getting a rundown on the suspect's normal times in and out of his first-floor flat, Gavin and Karalus went there early one afternoon that July. With Karalus standing watch on the sidewalk, Gavin went in using standard lock-picking equipment and installed a live-wire in a kitchen telephone receptacle. To Karalus' horror, "Joe P" made an unexpected quick

45

return home and was walking in the driveway on the side of the apartment building, prompting Karalus to walk slowly after him, so that if the suspect turned around and looked suspicious, Karalus could say he was going to visit a second floor neighbor.

As luck would have it, Gavin, who heard the suspect opening his kitchen door, quickly and quietly began opening the front door to the flat as Karalus quickly followed the suspect into the kitchen, grabbed a nearby chair and slammed it over his head, knocking him to the floor before fleeing out the back. Under an existing escape plan worked out before the job, Karalus and Gavin met up in the coffee shop of the nearby Millard Fillmore Hospital at Gates Circle, relieved at the success of the operation which paid off in worthwhile intelligence on stolen property shipment plans for several years before "Joe P" moved and the live wire was deactivated.

Furs-A-Plenty

Buffalo had a thriving underground fur business in the 1960s until the Forest Avenue Boys tapped into the phone lines of Magaddino's Arm and zeroed in on a Johnny Sacco-led multi-location business, netting upwards of $300,000 worth of furs stolen from Buffalo-area furriers by the end of 1967. While about $100,000 worth of furs stolen from the Sydney Gross shop on Broadway in November 1967 were destined to be sold to a Rochester, New York fur dealer by the Arm, the Boys' wiretaps set up the seizure of 71 furs, including a full-length ranch mink that carried a retail value of $5,000, that were recovered on Dec. 5, 1967 in the Arm's attic "store" on Buffalo's Amsterdam Avenue.

Like all the stolen furs recovered that month, the $5,000 mink, marked down by Magaddino's boys to $1,695, had its lining removed to allow the rival furrier who bought the stolen goods to attach his own labeled lining. Customers of the Amsterdam Avenue "fur shop," "shopped" in the store after midnight when it was open by invitation only, paying at most one-third of the normal retail prices of the furs sold there.

After the initial success early in December 1967, the Forest Avenue Boys learned through their wiretaps that Sacco had stored dozens of other stolen furs in a garage on Buffalo's Auburn Avenue. Zeroing in on that location, squad members Karalus and Eddie Palascak on a very rainy December 1967 night, drove to that garage. To their surprise they found the garage door open with furs hidden under a large tarp. Opting to rain on Sacco's parade, the two made sure no one was around and "stole" the furs and other stolen items they found in the garage which they sent for storage at the Troop A headquarters evidence room in Batavia under orders from Capt. Hank Williams. On December 22, 1967, Williams and Buffalo Police Chief of Detectives Ralph J. Degenhart showed the news media the stolen Auburn Street bounty—some $200,000 worth of furs, jewelry, silverware, glassware and cigarettes recovered from both that garage and in a subsequent raid on the Auburn Avenue house that belonged to Sacco.

Along with some more Sydney Gross stolen furs, the Forest Avenue Boys' "heist" recovered some $55,000 worth of silverware and glassware stolen from Buffalo's posh Pitt Petri store, $13,000 worth of street-sellable cigarette packs, a number of fur coats including a $13,000 full-length chinchilla coat and an electromagnetic drill used by Sacco and mob-linked safecrackers. Williams and FBI spokesman Wesson Campbell told the media that the electromagnetic drill was "a highly sophisticated tool and not one the average burglar uses." Further investigation confirmed that some of the stolen goods Sacco had been storing in the Auburn Avenue garage had come from out-of-town store thefts.

The morning after Karalus and Palascak "stole" all the stolen furs from Sacco's Auburn Avenue garage, the Forest Avenue Boys mob wires went wild with various lieutenants of Magaddino blaming Sacco and "Sam" Pieri for the loss of the goods and several suggesting an "assignment" be placed on the lives of both. Back at their anonymous headquarters at 400 Forest Avenue, the Boys had a lot of laughs that morning and celebrated with an extra cup of coffee, before they got back to work on the wires.

The Office

The Tunnel Job That Never Was

At the beginning of April 1967, the Boys picked up wires about the Arm's plan to tunnel under Niagara Street to break into what was then called a Manufacturers and Traders Trust Co. bank branch at 460 Niagara Street at the intersection with Hudson Street in Buffalo. It was supposed to be a major job for Thaddeus "The Goose" Wedalowski, a master Polish-American burglar. The Boys confirmed through their telephone tap that they had gotten the OK for the job from Magaddino's lieutenants. The plan called for payment of a bribe to a captain on the Buffalo police department to get a music permit for the house the boys rented across the street from the bank. The idea was that loud music coming from the house would cover the noise of the drilling being done to dig a tunnel across Niagara to break into the bank.

Gearing for a July 4th weekend heist, the Goose squad got special tools and had a truck ready to move dirt away from the tunnel site with Johnny Sacco recruiting "Frankie The Bug Man" and Butch, two master safe men from Cleveland to shut down the bank's alarm system and open the safe on the holiday weekend. The State Police Team was gearing up for the heist after getting wired confirmation that special tools, including drill bits and Canadian dynamite of the type preferred by mobsters throughout the northern states had been shipped to Buffalo for the job from Cleveland in an Erie County Election Board truck containing voting booths. The truck was driven by a mob-friendly employee. All the material for the bank heist was stored in a warehouse in anticipation of the bank job.

The Arm had a watchman checking on the warehouse to keep track of the tools but after weeks of planning for the July 4th job it was called off and the Boys never got a clear answer why the bank job planned by Sam Pieri, the Magaddino's contact with the gifted burglars in Cleveland, was cancelled. All that was clear after the abandoned 1967 bank job was that Magaddino's forces routinely "planned" many more jobs than they actually carried out. But the Boys confirmed through their wires that instead of the Buffalo bank job during the July 4 weekend in 1967, the Cleveland burglars, led as usual by a guy known to the Boys only as "Frankie The Bug Man" broke into three business safes in Utica and Rome, both in central New York.

The Fat Lady Sang

Through its live wires and bugs, the Forest Avenue Boys quickly realized Magaddino's Arm controlled the majority of the burglaries and thefts of valuable property throughout Western New York and a good part of the Canadian province of Ontario. Often Magaddino's lieutenants would place calls to the sophisticated fences in New York City that the Big Apple's five Mafia clans used. But that would entail splitting the profits, something Magaddino always found distasteful.

In the 1960s, Carrie M. Rapp, a/k/a, "The Fat Lady," ran an antique and second-hand shop she called Rapp Antiques in the 800 block of Buffalo's Broadway. Johnny Sacco, "Sam" Pieri and Thaddeus "The Goose" Wedalowski, a master burglar who lived down the street from her shop, made use of her store to fence a lot of stolen property according to the various live bugs and taps the Boys operated. Soon after the Boys began their clandestine efforts, it became clear that Sacco was running burglary and fencing operations for "Sam" Pieri and Joe Fino. A wire the Boys installed at the Fat Lady's shop confirmed she was moving stolen goods for the Arm all over the Eastern United States, much of it soon after the goods were stolen and brought to her shop.

Though Rapp, who also ran a restaurant on Buffalo's Howard Street, was never charged with complicity in the operations of Sacco or any other criminals, the then-70 year-old businesswoman was one of the suspects picked up in the last stolen property bust in 1972 based on the Boys' work. The Boys assumed "The Fat Lady" had few problems moving stolen goods out of her shop—something she did with military precision and speed—because she was protected both by Magaddino's legions and Buffalo police operating out of Precinct 8 near her business. Sacco and "Sam" Pieri were regularly heard by the Boys vouching for her prowess and Pieri seemed to be the source of the underworld "protection" that enabled her to keep large amounts of cash in her shop. With

Magaddino's Arm guarding her shop—and making sure Western New York's underworld knew that—armed robberies were never a concern for her.

The Boys learned that goods were moved out of "The Fat Lady's" shop by another woman, a truck driver who was always referred to on the wires as "Split Face." Though most of the mob loot delivered to "The Fat Lady's" shop was shipped out of state, the Boys confirmed that she was also selling weapons whose numbers had been filed off. Gamblers would come to her shop to sell property rather than using Magaddino's loan sharks. The Fat Lady was eventually corralled in an early 1972 State Police raid of mob-related stolen property cases that ended her underworld career. Then 70-years old and identified by the local news media as a suspect "in the antique business," she ended up with a slap on the wrist for felony stolen property charges lodged against her.

In addition to the Fat Lady, the Arm used several Buffalo area jewelry stores to dispose of stolen jewelry and watches. Sid Birzon and the less distinguished Stanley J. Senchowa, were heard by the Boys in monitoring the wires and taps. Senchowa ran Sench Jewelers at 401 Fillmore Avenue near Memorial Drive and had the approval to sell stolen items at his shop from both Sacco and Sam Pieri, according to the wires.

Based on information assembled by the Boys and painstaking surveillance efforts, Birzon, a wholesale jeweler who parlayed his skills as a diamond setter and salesman into a country-wide business and operated a highly-patronized jewelry store in downtown Buffalo for decades, was among 44 mob-linked suspects indicted by an Erie County, NY, grand jury in 1971 for possessing stolen jewelry taken two years earlier from the home of noted Buffalo area businessman Max B. E. Clarkson.

At his June 1971 arraignment Birzon, then 52, pleaded not guilty to first and second-degree criminal possession of stolen property and remained free on low bail. Ultimately he was acquitted because his high-powered attorney made mincemeat of the testimony of burglar-turned-snitch Gregory Parness.

The Office

Salli Boy

The Boys also zeroed in on Salvatore "Sam" Salli, once a leader of a notorious American-Canadian counterfeiting ring busted up in the early 1950s. In the 1960s—with counterfeiting still running through his blood—Salli was operating a pornography branch of the Magaddino empire from his home on West Avenue and using his hairdresser girlfriend Joy's house on Inwood Avenue. The Boys bugged both places. In the early 1950s Salli was defended in court by a noted Buffalo defense attorney quite familiar with representing organized crime figures—Anthony Manguso who ultimately became the head of the Buffalo city law department under Mayor Frank A. Sedita.

The Boys learned that Salli, who got a 10-year federal prison term in the early 1950s for his Buffalo-based nationwide counterfeiting operation, in the mid-1960s would frequently go to Joy's place to make calls about his pornography operations, feeling that was a "safe" call spot. The Boys focused on Salli's sales of porn through the managers of various Western New York businesses, including friends the Magaddino forces made in store-level operations of various supermarkets.

The Boys found from the Salli wires that Sam would drive to New York city two or three times a week to pick up at the Dixie Hotel reels of porn featuring women from Central and South America. The Boys opted not to tip off New York City police about Salli's regular trips there because their unit was so secret that their operation could have been exposed in court and their wires and live bugs would have become public—destroying their operation. Salli dealt with porn "customers" on his home phone and on his girlfriend's phone and on what he called "phone #6" at a laundry on Niagara Street and Hudson where he would hang out waiting for calls at specific times during the week. In addition to distributing porn through associates at Buffalo-area supermarkets and convenience stores, the Boys learned that Salli, who seemed to get along with anyone he ran into, sold many reels of porn to various members of Magaddino's Arm, local men's clubs and area law enforcement figures.

The Office

Ultimately busted because of all the information the Boys developed about his porn business, Salli's never-ending love of the counterfeiting trade landed him yet another federal prison term of two years in 1973 when Federal prosecutors in New York City nailed him and five others on conspiracy to distribute and sell counterfeit U.S. $50 and $100 bills nationwide.

Mr. Zoo

Not all the animals at the Buffalo, NY, Zoo lived in above ground cages or roamed its open air grounds in the late 1960s, the Forest Avenue Boys learned. Thanks to the connivance of Johnny Sacco, the Magaddino family's unofficial field marshal for its burglary brigade and nationwide stolen property fencing operations, the Zoo's underground tunnels under its main animal houses—used by Civil Defense officials to store emergency supplies designed to overcome any Cold War era nuclear attacks by the Soviet Union—for five years served as one of the major warehouses for Magaddino's vast array of stolen property.

The tunnels were where New York City area mobsters could make regular late-night visits to pick up goods and move them out of the area to other branches of La Cosa Nostra's off-the-books sales operations in the East. Already aware that Magaddino's forces controlled most of the stolen goods fencing operations in Western New York and Ontario, the Forest Avenue Boys began picking up indications in early 1968 on the John Sacco taps of both his home and the Talisman nightclub about stolen TVs and similar booty being taken to the Buffalo Zoo.

In early June 1968 Sacco started getting calls from a never-identified man who complained about his red truck being damaged by the trees he had to drive past at the Buffalo Zoo while delivering stolen silverware for storage. When that trucker began demanding more money Sacco could be heard telling the trucker to shut up because he was already making enough "bread" on his nighttime deliveries.

Finally Frenchy Rivard told Karalus to take his wife, Barbara, and their kids to the Zoo to look for trees that might have red vehicle paint on them as a result of the careless driving of that

The Office

Sacco "delivery man." On a warm Sunday afternoon in mid-June of that year Karalus took his family to the Zoo. While he walked with one daughter looking around the buildings at the front of the Zoo, Barbara took a different route around the buildings and within a few minutes ran to him saying she found two trees with red paint stains on them. The two paint-stained trees were near heavy steel doors leading into some sort of storage area and far enough apart so a good-sized truck could easily drive between them to get to and from the steel doors.

The Boys had long known Magaddino's Arm made use near the Zoo of Buffalo's Delaware Park Lake—a product of the city's famed Pan-American Exposition of 1901 where President McKinley was assassinated—to dispose of unwanted "items." The Boys had thought little about that aspect of the Real Teflon Don's empire until the unidentified delivery man's complaints to Sacco about the damage to his "red truck." Also in 1968, the Sacco wires began airing references to a "Mr. Zoo" and the Boys used mob informants to confirm that "Mr. Zoo" was a Zoo employee named Donald Fusco. They confirmed that Fusco had ready access to the underground tunnels, referred to by some as "the catacombs," near those red paint-marked trees at the front of the Zoo and its animal house.

Courier Express photo of the raid on the Buffalo Zoo. From left to right: George Karalus, DA Mike Dillon and Captain Hank Williams (standing.)

With the Cold War with the Soviet Union still very hot in the 1960s, the Zoo's underground storage area was used to warehouse blankets, first aid equipment, cots, gas masks and barrels of fresh water all of which would be available when the first Soviet nuclear bombs began falling on the nearby Niagara Falls. The Falls, one of the Seven Wonders of the World, had long been considered one of the prime targets of a nuclear attack designed to paralyze the country's energy resources in the heavily-populated Northeastern section of the country. The Forest Avenue Boys saw that the rear of the animal house allowed trucks to be backed up to the tunnels for the quick movement of stolen goods into and out of that rent-free mob "warehouse." The Boys found that the Magaddino Arm had been using the water barrels in its free underground storage site to store stolen diamonds kept in waterproof bags with strings attached so that they could be quickly removed for shipment to the mob family's fences throughout the Eastern United States.

After a year-long formal investigation into at least five years of mob use of the Zoo tunnels as a stolen property shipping point—thanks to the Forest Avenue Boys' wiretaps—Capt. Hank Williams, the Boys' boss in the State Police Bureau of Criminal Investigation, and Erie County, NY, District Attorney Michael F. Dillon in June, 1971, launched a raid with 145 officers into the Magaddino mob's multi-million-dollar stolen property operation. That raid targeted the possible recovery of autos, trucks, boats, jewelry, art work, cigarettes and scores of other items. The June 7, 1971 raid on the mob's Buffalo Zoo warehouse took place as hundreds of Buffalo school children toured the Zoo that day unaware of the dramatic events underway in the hot, humid and dimly-lit tunnels under them.

However, only some stolen diamonds were recovered from the Zoo tunnels because Sacco associates on the Buffalo Police Department payroll had likely tipped him off to the plans for the raid. Diving operations into the murky waters of the Delaware Park Lake near the Zoo later recovered a wall safe and sterling silver trays. Initially 37 suspects were arrested on burglary, robbery, extortion and related crimes. Thanks to the work of the Forest Avenue Boys, the taxpaying public learned—through announcement by other law enforcement agents—of the mob's systematic use of the Zoo tunnels.

What started out as a major law enforcement effort against the Zoo stolen goods storehouse almost ended in tragedy as Dillon—who ultimately became one of New York State's top judges—was touring the Zoo tunnels with Captain Williams and several of the Forest Avenue Boys late in the afternoon of June 7, 1971 after the raid. The paw of a brown bear who was obviously angered by all the underground noise and flash of news media cameras came within inches of the district attorney's head as he was being pulled to safety. After the Zoo raid, the Forest Avenue Boys began hearing dozens of angry calls between Magaddino senior associates—all accusing each other of selling out to the law and in the end revealing the vast extent of the Magaddino family's burglary and fencing operations.

Because of the efficiency of Magaddino's fencing operations and its ties to various Western New York law enforcement officials, by the time of the June 1971 raid, with the exception of some stolen diamonds, the Zoo underground "warehouse" had been drained of all the high-priced items Sacco's largely drug-addicted burglars had stolen from some of the Buffalo area's most fashionable homes and businesses. Credible informants had spoken of the millions of dollars worth of stolen property that had graced the Mob's underground "warehouse" prior to the raid but by the June 1971 raid the "warehouse" was nearly empty. "Mr. Zoo," Donald Fusco, was one of 44 persons indicted by a holdover grand jury that had looked into hundreds of burglaries linked to the Zoo "warehouse."

As the alleged "warehouse keeper" for the Mob, Fusco was indicted for criminal possession of a felony-sized quantity of cigarettes and watches stolen from Buffalo-area drug stores and business warehouses and postage stamps stolen from a North Tonawanda post office just north of Buffalo in 1968. In March 1972, Fusco pleaded guilty to criminal possession of stolen property, sentenced to five years probation and ordered to pay restitution. After the city transferred the Zoo operation to a non-profit group that still runs it, Fusco, probably because of mob-ties to the Buffalo city government, just ended up being transferred to another city department until he retired years later.

The Office

The Two-Fisted Painter

The Boys long suspected Magaddino's troops took advantage of the international luster and art world connections of Buffalo's Anthony J. "Tony" Sisti (1901-1983) because of frequent references made by Magaddino's men to a Buffalo boxer-turned-painter on mob wiretaps. Sisti had studied at the Royal Academy of Fine Arts in Florence, Italy from 1926 to 1931, earning a doctorate in painting. In 1918 he won New York State's Golden Gloves bantamweight championship and became a professional boxer, retiring with an 85-15 won-lost record.

The Boys suspected but were never able to establish that Magaddino had an actual criminal deal with the renowned Buffalo artist and art dealer to fence stolen art work through the nationally-known art studio and gallery that the classically-trained painter, collector and patron of the arts ran on Buffalo's Linwood Avenue from 1938 until his death. Sisti periodically sold paintings that Magaddino's senior officers like John Montana asked him to peddle, seemingly unaware of the true origins of that art work.

The Boys suspected Sisti of selling some artwork stolen by Magaddino's forces primarily because of his keen ability to select good art and his seemingly uncanny ability to "discover" valuable paintings brought to him by truck drivers and other working people. Born in New York City's Greenwich Village and credited with pioneering the artistic and cultural rebirth of Buffalo's Allentown, a minor Greenwich Village in its own right, Sisti actually hit the big time financially by being one of the next-door Allentown neighbors of then-struggling watercolorist Charles Burchfield. Long before Burchfield became the talk of the international art world, Sisti purchased many of his paintings and exhibited them at his gallery to provide the near-poverty-stricken Burchfield with money to pay his rent and buy food for his family.

In 1958, Sisti helped his Allentown neighbors organize an outdoor art festival, serving as the first chairman of what became the Allentown Art Festival held each June. In 1979, Sisti donated 25 of Burchfield's by-then nearly priceless paintings, eight Burchfield drawings and 25 of his own paintings which included portraits of tenor Enrico Caruso and President Franklin D. Roosevelt to the Burchfield Center at Buffalo State College in Buffalo, New York. That center grew into the famed Burchfield Penney Art Center alongside the Buffalo State campus.

In 1981, the City of Buffalo named the Tony Sisti Park in his honor near the intersection of Franklin and North Streets. When the Burchfield Penny Art Center was opened on Elmwood Avenue on the Buffalo State College campus in 2009, one of that museum's main floor galleries was named after Sisti.

The Boys' suspicions about Sisti and his possible links to the Magaddino crime family were belatedly dispelled as a result of what turned into seven nasty years of court fights launched by one of Sisti's two daughters after the death of the Buffalo artistic legend in December 1983 and the death of his beloved wife Carmella, better known as "Nellie" four months later.

The Magaddino of the Art World

Sisti may have been wasted time for the Boys, but in 1968 they managed to assist in the recovery of a number of paintings, including a priceless Rembrandt and they spoiled the trifecta of thefts engineered by Russell DeCicco, a long-time Magaddino soldier and periodic federal snitch whose information proved to be on a par with that of Johnny Sacco in terms of its relative uselessness. After DeCicco's life in Buffalo became worth less than a "plugged nickel" in the mid-1970s, he went on to reinvent himself as a Florida antique dealer and head of a vicious South Florida home-invasion gang.

In 1968, there was a string of major art heists. These included the Jan. 31, 1968 theft of Rembrandt's majestic 41-by-38 inch "Portrait of a Young Man" from the George Eastman Museum in Rochester; the Aug. 21, 1968 theft of $1.4 million worth of paintings and sculpture from the Bradford, Pa. mansion of the late oil millionaire and well-known art collector T. Edward Hanley and his flamboyant widow Tullah Innes Hanley; and the theft of about $50,000 worth of largely modern art from the Buffalo mansion of banker and nationally known modern art collector Seymour H.

Knox on Sept. 8, 1968. The Boys would periodically pick up calls about Russell DeCicco and his eagerness to sell these items.

The Boys' work led to the recovery of the Hanley loot eight days after the break-in and later to the arrests of DeCicco, his wife, Renee, and Gregory Parness and Louis (Markus) Mavrakis, both 22 of Buffalo—thanks also to the paid FBI informant work of Parness' older brother Paul H. Parness who ended up in federal protective custody. The Rembrandt was the pride of the Rochester museum which was located in the former 37-room mansion of the late George Eastman, founder of the Eastman Kodak Co., and was operated by the University of Rochester. The Boys passed on a tip to a New York State Police crew under the command of Maj. Harold Muller of Troop B upstate about DeCicco's plans to sell the Rembrandt for $250,000 to eager buyers who would pick it up in Plattsburgh in northern New York State.

DeCicco and two other men, one from Rochester and one from Chicago, were arrested by the Muller team when they arrived at the Clinton County Airport in Plattsburgh about 7 p.m. Oct. 15, 1968 with the painting.

The Plattsburgh arrest of the often-arrested DeCicco came two months after he took part in the August 1968 burglary of the Bradford, Pennsylvania home of Tullah Innes Hanley in which 14 masterpiece paintings and two bronze statuettes valued at about $1.4 million had been stolen. The work of the Boys and Paul Parness led to the quick recovery of the Hanley collection which included a $600,000 Picasso and a $450,000 Cezanne. The Knox modern art was never recovered, forcing a major insurance company to cut a large check to the Knox estate.

In June, 1969, DeCicco, his wife and Greg Parness and Mavrakis got federal prison terms for the Hanley thefts but after DeCicco spent about two years at the Leavenworth Federal Prison, the convictions were overturned due to prosecutorial errors during the Buffalo trial. After his release from Leavenworth, DeCicco, thanks to Fred Randaccio, was put on the payroll of the Buffalo loansharking and bookmaking operations run for Magaddino's Arm by mobster Albert M. "Babe" Billitteri.

The crafty DeCicco also hooked up with Russell A. Bufalino, northern Pennsylvania mob boss and a Magaddino cousin, in a gang war over control of the vending-machine industries in Syracuse and Binghamton, New York. DeCicco became a government witness against Bufalino but the aging Don and 14 others were all acquitted in 1974 of conspiracy, extortion and related charges linked the gang war. A federal task force had relied on the questionable informant work of DeCicco and Joseph T. Zito, a former mobster in the Batavia area of Western New York.

Looking to feather his nest any way he could, DeCicco began getting paid as an FBI informant in 1971. He hooked up with Zito and Gregory Parness in 1975 in a federal challenge to "Babe" Billitteri's bid for an early parole on his 5-year sentence for mob-related conspiracy to loan shark. After being admitted to the Federal Witness Protection Program in the early 1970s, DeCicco testified before the grand jury that indicted Buffalo mobster Dominic A. Tascarella Jr. for the 1972 gangland-style murder of his former counterfeiting ally Steven Hasselbeck who had become a Secret Service informant and witness in a pending counterfeiting case.

While sleeping in a second floor apartment on Buffalo's West Side on March 20, 1972, Hasselbeck, 22, was shot seven times at close range with a .45-caliber revolver. After testifying before the grand jury about the wires he was allegedly wearing while talking to Tascarella about the Hasselbeck murder, DeCicco fled for his life to Florida after hearing about an "assignment" on his own life in Buffalo. Arrested by federal task force operatives in Miami and returned to Buffalo, DeCicco testified at Tascarella's October 1975 state court murder trial, admitting on the stand that while he was on the FBI payroll as an informant in the case, he had made $50,000 selling $6 million worth of stolen securities. Tascarella was acquitted of the Hasselbeck murder.

Returning to Florida, DeCicco changed his name to Russell DeFranco and posed as an antiques dealer through his Orange Mill Antique Shop in Dania Beach near Ft. Lauderdale. DeCicco, then living in a modest house in Hollywood, Fla., became the leader of what authorities described after his arrest in the mid-1980s as a vicious South Florida gang of home invaders who staged more than 40 home invasions. The invasions were called "wrap-ups" because victims found at the break-in scenes were routinely wrapped up in rope and duct tape with the mouths taped shut as the burglars ransacked the dwellings. The burglars would torture and threaten victims until they told them the combinations to safes and hiding places of valuables including Peruvian tapestries, Persian rugs and silver and crystal antiques.

DeCicco ultimately pled guilty to racketeering charges carrying a possible 30-year Federal prison term for providing his gang with the addresses of his wealthy business customers and then fencing their loot which he let them hide in his Hollywood, Florida home. Searches of both the Florida prison system and the Federal prison system online records produced no information on either a Russell DeCicco or a Russell Defranco. This suggests that even as DeCicco neared his golden years after a life of crime that began with his first arrest in Buffalo in 1953, he may have managed to connive his way back into the Federal Witness Protection Program.

Birzon Agonistes

The Forest Avenue Boys' intercepts of mob talks morphed into investigations of an estimated $20 million worth of burglaries staged by mob associates in the Buffalo area in the late 1960s and early 1970s including the homes of world-renowned author and Buffalo native Taylor Caldwell, Buffalo Evening News publisher James H. Righter, millionaire banker and art patron Seymour Knox, retired Bethlehem Steel plant manager Robert S. Bennett and dozens of other local notables.

The investigations prompted by the Boys' intercepts resulted in charges being lodged in June 1971 against 44 individuals including Buffalo area wholesale jeweler Sidney Birzon for allegedly dealing in stolen goods through Magaddino's then number two man or underboss Joseph M. Fino and Fino's predecessor as underboss, "Sam" Pieri. Fino and Pieri were also arrested in that June 1971 roundup along with Sammie Sacco and Carrie Rapp, the "Fat Lady" antique and used property businesswoman long suspected of trafficking in the Magaddino Arm's stolen goods.

The Boys had been able to confirm that Sacco-supervised goons had broken into Knox's posh Oakland Place mansion in 1968 stealing paintings, jewelry and cash, none of which was ever recovered. Knox was chairman emeritus of Buffalo-based Marine Midland Bank and a retired director of the F. W. Woolworth company. Thanks to underwater searches triggered by the Boys wiretaps, a safe stolen from newspaper publisher Righter's Buffalo mansion was ultimately recovered, empty, in the Buffalo River.

Birzon parlayed his skills as a diamond setter and salesman into a downtown Buffalo wholesale jewelry business and in 1961 co-founded the Fantasy Island Amusement Park on Buffalo's island suburb of Grand Island. He was charged in June 1971 with first and second-degree criminal possession of stolen property linked to a $10,000 emerald stolen from the home of Buffalo industrialist Max B. E. Clarkson in April 1969 by Magaddino's Arm.

Following a week-long State Supreme Court jury trial in Buffalo in February, 1973, Birzon, then 54, was found not guilty of criminally possessing the stolen Clarkson emerald. During that jury trial Gregory Parness, then 26 and an admitted burglar, testified that he had sold the 23 and one-half carat emerald to Birzon. Parness also claimed he had done business with the later-nationally known jeweler on several occasions involving stolen jewelry. The jury didn't believe the unsavory-looking Parness. Birzon took the witness stand in his own defense and admitted knowing Parness and having done business with him in the past. But Birzon categorically denied ever buying the stolen Clarkson emerald—never recovered by authorities—or any other stolen goods from Parness. Birzon's lawyer Charles J. McDonough, then a prominent Buffalo defense attorney, denounced Parness, telling the jury that as an admitted crook Parness' testimony about selling Birzon the stolen emerald in May 1969 was "incredible."

Birzon went on to develop a profitable nationwide wholesale jewelry business and was publicly recognized for his contributions to bond drives financing the nation of Israel. He died in Florida on Dec. 1, 2008 at the age of 90.

The Cadillac Reef

Following tips developed by BCI Investigator Joe Cooley with help from Karalus and with wires the Forest Avenue Boys had on Joe Fino and Nino Magaddino, a multi-year probe of the Arm's highly lucrative stolen car business in the summer of 1972 led to the recovery of some 60 stolen vehicles in the murky waters off a long-abandoned pier at the foot of Buffalo's Michigan Avenue. Divers from the Buffalo Police assisted State Police with Buffalo Harbormaster Thomas Reardon using sounding equipment installed on his craft to close in on the watery grave of that booty.

The Boys' wires picked up Fino listening as Magaddino himself boasted in 1966 about how stolen cars for the Mob would be "bigger than drugs." The Boys also listened in fascination to Magaddino talking to Fino about how much he enjoyed having his forces stealing police cars, both for their value in providing chop shops with various automotive parts and just to irritate his opponents on the other side of the law.

Cooley's investigative work confirmed that the Mob was using several Buffalo-area junkyards to handle stolen cars and using reliable fences to sell vehicles and vehicle parts outside the Buffalo area. In 1967, the Forest Avenue Boys, based on their Fino wires, arrested several junkyard operators, beginning the process that ended a Mob-overseen auto theft ring that had been generating six-figure profits over several years in the late 1960s. It turned out that Fino and his aides had recruited street thugs to steal cars in return for just enough money to keep them high on drugs and booze. Working with the Buffalo Police auto theft unit, the Forest Avenue Boys provided BCI officials with information that led to the June 1, 1972 start of dredging operations off the foot of Main Street. That led to the recovery of scores of stolen vehicles dumped off a long-abandoned pier. Among the recovered booty were the private automobiles of a former Buffalo Bills football player and a Buffalo police officer.

While the "Cadillac Reef" probe led to the recovery of over 100 stolen vehicles, the Boys were never able to pinpoint their suspicions that at least one Buffalo area police officer was in cahoots with Magaddino's Arm in arranging the successful theft of heavy-duty construction site equipment, including forklifts and trucks shipped from Western New York to New York City, apparently on the New York State Thruway, for eventual shipment to the Middle East where there were ready buyers.

The Office

Westfield Jimmy and the Cleveland Mob

After confirming early on that "Sam" Pieri would regularly drive to the Mayfield Heights area of Cleveland to talk with the heads of the Cleveland mob, the Forest Avenue Boys set up a wire in a motel that Magaddino "lieutenant" James "Westfield Jimmy" Salamone operated at the New York-Pennsylvania border. Salamone, one of Magaddino's key Pennsylvania operatives, controlled the illegal numbers racket in Erie, Pennsylvania. The wire on "Westfield Jimmy's" led to the periodic seizures of stolen property Magaddino was shipping to Cleveland for sale or that the Cleveland mob was trucking to Buffalo and Pennsylvania for sale by either Magaddino's men or Russell Bufalino.

Bufalino was the Magaddino relative and former Buffalo auto mechanic who built a Northwestern Pennsylvania-based crime organization which he had taken over in 1959 and built into what was described by the Pennsylvania Crime Commission in 1980 as possibly "the most powerful Cosa Nostra family" in the Northeast with its influence extending into Central and Western New York after the death of Magaddino and into areas of New York City once controlled by the late Vito Genovese.

Other Agencies

The Boys only fully trusted the Royal Canadian Mounted Police to receive mob information with no fears of it being forwarded to the wrong people. But they also came to trust Pennsylvania state authorities, avoiding Ohio State troopers like the plague when it came to sharing intelligence.

The Boys felt confident in dealing with the police departments in the Buffalo suburbs of Amherst and the Town of Tonawanda but they never trusted either the Buffalo Police Department or the police department in its suburb of Cheektowaga where mob-run gambling operations were staged in the 800 block of Rein Road literally in the plain sight of town officials.

The Forest Avenue Boys routinely picked up references to Cheektowaga, New York, and its government officials in the

The Office

Magaddino-connected wires and live hookups and their work sparked subsequent and costly investigations of Cheektowaga government officials and workers which ended with a few convictions in the 1970s after the Elmwood Avenue operation had been shut down.

You **Can** Watch City Hall

The Boys' set up surveillance of Buffalo City Hall in the late 1960's, making use of a room provided by the parish administration behind the Sanctuary of St. Anthony of Padua Roman Catholic Church at 160 Court Street and running along South Elmwood Avenue right behind Buffalo's City Hall. The Boys soon began noticing master stolen property fencer Johnny Sacco, Joe Fino and other Magaddino affiliates periodically entering City Hall through that back entrance. LaDuca was among those regularly spotted entering City Hall through one of its back doors on South Elmwood Avenue across from the church.

The Boys quickly confirmed that Anthony Manguso, Mayor Sedita's Corporation Counsel, was the Buffalo government official LaDuca regularly met at City Hall. Manguso was a former skilled defense lawyer whose clients once included a number of Magaddino's boys. On a hot summer day in 1969, Karalus called Manguso's City Hall office and asked to speak to the corporation counsel while LaDuca was in with him. Claiming to be an anonymous "friend" Karalus told Manguso "I just want to tell you the state troopers have a truck taking pictures of City Hall."

Manguso said "What. Who is this?" "Just a friend," Karalus replied.

"What color is it," Manguso asked of the truck.

"White," the "friend" replied.

"White. Thanks for the call. State Police, are you sure?" Manguso asked as LaDuca obviously was listening intently.

"Yes," Karalus replied.

"Ok. Thanks," Manguso said as he hung up.

Moments later LaDuca was spotted scurrying out the back door of City Hall. LaDuca's frequent visits to Manguso's City Hall office never generated any useable intelligence about mob activities and for a time Maury Gavin who had come to know LaDuca felt he was on the verge of "turning" LaDuca into a state police informant. But that was never to be.

During riots in Buffalo by African-Americans in 1967 and by college students in 1970, LaDuca was heard talking on the Camellia tap about how the Real Teflon Don was upset at how the street demonstrations and threats of physical damage had brought out more police officers to deal with the rioters and ended up crimping the Arm's money-making ability during those periods.

LaDuca would also talk on his Camellia office phone about how Magaddino was pleased to know Sam Pieri had been contacted by business owners during those riots in 1967 and 1970 to arrange for "protection" of their businesses. LaDuca spoke during those Camellia taps about how Pieri and Roy "The Fisherman" Carlisi, another of Magaddino's top officials, ended up getting a cut out of many business repair jobs linked to the physical damage inflicted on Buffalo stores and offices during those riots.

LaDuca's business telephone talks also disclosed that Magaddino had put out the word that none of his soldiers were to interfere with police dealing with rioters. Magaddino, the LaDuca taps disclosed, was also against business ties with the young "hippie" troublemakers and "niggers" dealing in drugs on the streets. Like Don Corleone, the Real Teflon Don felt street drugs were "bad for us," LaDuca would tell his callers.

The Buffalo City Hall surveillance proved to the Boys that Anthony Manguso played a major role in keeping Mayor Sedita from falling under the control of Magaddino and the Mafia. Manguso's former work as a well-respected Buffalo criminal defense attorney for a number of Magaddino's associates including counterfeiter and pornography pusher Salvatore "Sam" Salli and similar mob foot soldiers made it easy for him to deflect LaDuca.

Manguso had routinely but honestly dealt with the likes of LaDuca and Salli during his nearly three decades as a private lawyer from 1928 to 1957 when he began what proved to be his distinguished career in public office. A boyhood chum of Buffalo Mayor Frank A. Sedita, Manguso's first stint at public office came in May 1957 when New York Gov. Averell Harriman appointed him an Erie County Court judge to replace a recently resigned office holder. Manguso, the son of a West Side Buffalo butcher, had lost his first political campaign when he ran for the Buffalo-based Erie County Court in 1955. He only lasted seven months in his gubernatorially-appointed judgeship, losing in the November 1957 elections.

Because Sedita long ago had come to appreciate Manguso's legal skills, he appointed him his corporation counsel, making him the city government's top lawyer in 1958 at the age of 52. A self-described "public service enthusiast" Manguso was an unsuccessful Democratic Party candidate for New York State Supreme Court in 1960. He stepped down as Mayor Sedita's Corporation Counsel in 1962 but when Sedita recaptured the mayoralty in 1965, he made sure that the day he took office again on Jan. 1, 1966, Manguso began his second term as corporation counsel. He kept the job until he retired shortly before his 70th birthday in January 1975 under Buffalo Mayor Stanley M. Makowski.

Manguso was the likely reason his boyhood pal Sedita never got swept into Magaddino's underworld. Manguso craftily dealt in the 1960s with LaDuca and other associates of the Real Teflon Don, relying on his workplace-gathered knowledge of how to avoid being sucked into the corruption Magaddino and his henchmen labored to inflict on as many levels of government as they could.

Even after officially retiring as Buffalo government's top lawyer, Manguso continued his public service. He worked as an unpaid lawyer for the Buffalo Common Council, the city's law-making body, during a Federal Court school integration and financing case in the late 1970s. He also kept busy in the late 1970s heading a citizens committee challenging efforts to downsize the Buffalo Common Council.

CheektaVegas Danny

The Boys had long been suspicious of Danny Weber, a former Cheektowaga police detective sergeant who later ran for office. Weber was appointed to an unexpired term on the town council in 1958 as a Liberal and as a Republican was town supervisor from 1963 through 1975 when he was indicted on extortion charges. He was stricken with a cerebral hemorrhage but recovered and served as a Democratic town supervisor from 1983 through 1987. Though Weber called attention to himself by his strong public positions on a wide range of issues, including his unsuccessful efforts in the 1980s against auto seat belt laws, he oversaw the township's most explosive period of growth.

A World War II vet and former postal worker and home construction firm operator, Weber was twice cleared in court of government extortion charges after trials in 1975 and 1977. Though the Forest Avenue Boys never trusted Weber, guessing but unable to confirm his friendship with many of Magaddino's upper level lieutenants, Weber was honored by the Erie County Legislature in 1994 as it named the county's Fire Training Academy in Cheektowaga for him.

The Boys long thought that if they had just been kept together and refocused on Cheektowaga, their efforts would have either led to a mini-Watergate style government scandal or spared taxpayers a lot of wasted law enforcement and court expenses.

Office Politics

While the Forest Avenue Boys worked together like a well-oiled machine for nearly a decade, there were the usual personality "problems" between team members. Karalus regretted his inability to find out why Maury Gavin never truly trusted either Frenchy Rivard or Hank Williams. It seemed to have something to do with the fact that as team leader Frenchy had readily agreed to supply Williams, and through Williams, Erie County, NY, District Attorney Mike Dillon and the FBI—which no one on the secret squad ever fully trusted—with copies of transcripts of its secret wiretaps and bugging operations.

The success of the Buffalo unit was such that its Sicilian-language translator, Trooper Anthony "Tony" Dirienz was recruited in the early 1970s for similar duty with undercover units in New York City.

In the long-run, the wisdom of Hank Williams' decision to let the FBI, and through that agency all federal law enforcement, in on the inner workings of the Magaddino empire paid off, though the ham-fisted efforts of the G-Men meant the Magaddino empire wasn't shut down until long after the death of the Real Teflon Don.

As commander of state police forces dealing with the 1971 Attica prison riot, Williams took the public blame for the deaths of guards and inmates after New York Governor Rockefeller ordered a retaking of the prison. Williams was a lieutenant colonel in command of the State Police Bureau of Criminal Investigation at the time of his death in 1986 and his inspiration of a generation of state troopers and his championing of the use of science and technology in the investigation of crimes prompted the New York State Legislature in 1997 to name the new State Police lab, the Forensic Investigative Center in Albany, after Williams.

The Church Committee

Unlike the efforts of ultimately-disgraced New York Governor Eliot Spitzer to misuse the New York State Police for political gain against his chief political foe in the 21st Century, the Forest Avenue Boys' groundbreaking penetration of the Magaddino empire and related Buffalo criminal activity provided the FBI and other federal and state agencies with important knowledge about Mob thinking and planning in general and on specific jobs which survived even U.S. Sen. Frank Church's attack on U.S. intelligence operations in the 1970s. Church's efforts damaged the country's intelligence-gathering for a generation.

Spitzer used State Police travel records in 2007 to try to embarrass his political foes including his chief Republican Party foe State Senate Majority Leader Joseph L. Bruno of Brunswick, who was ultimately convicted of unrelated crimes. Spitzer resigned the governorship on March 17, 2008 following the public disclosure of his repeated use of a high-priced prostitution ring, but his use of the New York State Police for political spying publicly damaged law enforcement. Spitzer's successor, Gov. David A. Paterson in 2010 further sullied the reputation of the State Police by getting some of its troops involved in his ill-advised efforts to intervene in a domestic violence case involving a close aide.

Forgotten amid all that 21st Century turmoil was the ground-breaking role the New York State Police played in uncovering the nationwide Mafia crime network in 1957 and the Forest Avenue Boys' ground-breaking penetration into the inner-workings of the Magaddino crime family.

3. The Real Teflon Don

After the Forest Avenue Boys were ordered to take over the FBI's illegal bugging of Stefano "The Undertaker" Magaddino's Niagara Falls funeral business, it quickly became clear why the illiterate but highly intelligent and ruthless Sicilian died a very wealthy and never-convicted businessman on July 19, 1974 after 52 years of running the Buffalo-based mob family as one of the founders of and later the elder statesman of La Cosa Nostra. What became known to lawmen as Magaddino's Arm, his family-run crime empire, had tentacles that went north to Toronto, east to Utica, New York, west to Cleveland and the Ohio Valley and south through family ties to Pittsburgh.

Stefano was born on Oct. 10, 1891 into the upper echelons of Sicilian organized crime. He and his brothers, the later-murdered Pietro and Antonino (the Nino who became the field marshal of his lucrative American crime empire) were born to Giuseppe Magaddino, the Mafia Don of their native Castellammare del Golfo in Trapani Province, Sicily.

What came to be known as the Mafia or in America La Cosa Nostra began about seven centuries ago as a Sicilian organization that worked to protect the rights and holdings of Sicilians then under the control of the invading French who plundered the island with little regard for its residents. While initially formed to protect the populous from their French overlords, the militaristic organization began turning on fellow Sicilians. By the beginning of the 20th Century as Sicilians like the Magaddinos began emigrating to the United States in large numbers—a number of them already stamped with the Mafia code, they first organized in America as the

Black Hand, again touting themselves as the protectors of fellow immigrants but really just getting payments from immigrant merchants and businessmen so those "donors" could avoid experiencing "trouble" from the Black Hand.

Gambling, illegal numbers businesses and prostitution produced illegal revenues for years for what later morphed into the Mafia. The Volstead Act of 1919, banning alcohol sales in the states, was like manna from heaven for Magaddino and his Mafia cohorts eager to quench the national thirst for alcoholic beverages regardless of any paper documents adopted in Washington, D.C. and declared the law of the land by Congress.

God Bless America

Stefano Magaddino and his brother Nino had left Sicily after their older brother Pietro—after whom Stefano named his own son—was killed in 1916 as their family's clan warfare with Felice Buccellato's family escalated. Both in the Old World and the New the Magaddino brothers' family ties to the Bonanno and Bonventre crime families came in handy. When the Magaddino siblings sailed from their native Sicily, they did so with reputations as much-feared armed thieves and extortionists in their native land. Ultimately one of Pietro's alleged killers, Carmello Caizzo, was murdered in Brooklyn by Bartolo Fontana, who first disclosed the existence of "The Good Killers" gang to the New York Police Department's famed "Italian Squad" as he tried to buy his way out of a prison term.

Stefano and Nino and many others from Castellammare Del Golfo initially moved into the Williamsburg section of Brooklyn whose crime boss in the early 1900s was the Magaddinos' uncle, Vito Bonventre. A well-known Brooklyn baker, Bonventre was founder of the Good Killers gang of assassins. Stefano became one of the Good Killers' most feared and successful members. The powerfully-built Stefano had quickly acquired a reputation as a hardened killer, giving him a powerful and wealthy underworld presence much beyond his uncle's Roebling Street bakery near the Brooklyn Bridge.

The Real Teflon Don

Legend had it that Vito Bonventre formed the Good Killers in 1907 following the murder of a Bonventre clan chief whose dismembered body had been left in a bag on a Williamsburg street corner. As is frequently the case with Mafia legends, there was also talk of the Bonventre clan martyr having been unceremoniously dumped and burned to a crisp in one of the family's own bakery ovens. Legend also had it that Vito Bonventre had his slain kinsman's dismembered remains ceremonially brought to his Roebling Street bakery and placed piece by piece into his hot coal-fired brick oven as his associates gathered around as a display of their respect for their fallen comrade. It was out of that clan "tragedy" that the Good Killers motto—"Li Bruceremo!"—"We will burn you" Cairo, Ill.—reportedly developed.

Though Stefano Magaddino arrived in the United States speaking little English as well as being illiterate—which he remained for his long life—he had arrived here with a Sicilian reputation of being skilled in the use of guns and knives, a skill he displayed in the long-running blood feud between his kin, who included the Bonventre and Bonanno families and clans connected to the Buccellato family, a number of whom also migrated to the U.S. His skills as a warrior quickly transformed him from a seemingly coarse country bumpkin into a wealthy Mafia hit man for the Good Killers of Brooklyn. The Good Killers were reputedly involved in several hundred never-solved murders throughout the eastern section of the country and as far west as Colorado. They became known for their efficiency in killing their enemies and disposing of their bodies.

Vito Bonventre became wealthy bootlegging during Prohibition while serving as underboss to New York Mafia Kingpin Salvatore Maranzano. On July 15, 1930 the 55-year-old Bonventre was gunned down outside his own garage by a hit man affiliated with Giuseppe "Joe The Boss" Masseria, head of what later became known as the Genovese crime family. But the gunman was never identified or prosecuted. "Joe The Boss" was assassinated in one of his favorite Coney Island restaurants under the orders of Charles "Lucky" Luciano who was dining with him on April 15, 1931 until he went to the bathroom just before the gunmen stormed in and sprayed Masseria with bullets.

The Real Teflon Don

Uncle Vito's murder and the June 1930 murder of Gaspar Milazzo, another major Castellammarese clansman in a Detroit fish market, are considered by many to be the start of the Mafia's bloody Castellammarese War, since both killings supposedly had been orchestrated by Masseria, the Manhattan-based rival of both. By the start of the 1920s, Stefano Magaddino had gotten revenge on the Buccellato clan and that led to his arrest in Brooklyn in 1921 as a fugitive from justice in connection with the murder of a Buccellato man in Avon, New Jersey. A thug named Bartolo Fontana had became a police informant and made Stefano a target of New York City Police's famed "Italian Squad" which arrested him in 1921. During that brief jailing, Stefano ran into Fontana and screamed out to him the Sicilian phrase for "I'll burn you up for this." As he began assaulting Fontana, police beat Stefano to the floor with nightsticks.

The 1921 arrest and Stefano's brief jailing marked the only time the Real Teflon Don ever spent behind bars during what proved to be his bloody and violent sixty year American crime career. After being cleared of the Avon murder charge in the summer of 1921, Magaddino and his Brooklyn crime ally Gaspar Milazzo were both shot and wounded as they walked out of a Brooklyn store, prompting a retaliation that cost several more Buccellato men their lives and prompted Magaddino to relocate to Buffalo and then to Niagara Falls in 1922. Milazzo headed for Detroit.

Antonino, considerably less powerful physically than Stefano but more socially flamboyant, joined him in Niagara Falls and remained one of his top lieutenants until his own death in 1971 from natural causes. Once in the Buffalo area, the powerfully-built Magaddino became a key operative and a feared enforcer for the Mafia family of "Old Joe" DiCarlo, becoming such a feared member of that group that when DiCarlo died unexpectedly in 1922—of natural causes—DiCarlo's underboss Angelo "Buffalo Bill" Palmeri let Magaddino assume control of the family. He was appreciative of Magaddino's drive and no doubt was aware that when Magaddino had been a member of his uncle's Brooklyn gang of killers that bakery-linked group's motto had been "Li Bruceremo!'—WE WILL BURN YOU!

The Real Teflon Don

Ironically, Palmeri, who had emigrated from Castellammare del Golfo to the Buffalo area in 1908 or 1909 as an already wealthy and well-known Sicilian mobster, is credited by many as the mobster who actually formed the Italian-American crime family which DiCarlo and then Magaddino took over with his blessing. Legend has it that Palmeri assumed command as crime boss in Buffalo's Little Italy area of a group of Black Hand extortionists soon after he arrived, extorting protection money from Italian merchants including food vendors and pushcart businessmen as well as from pimps, prostitutes and drug dealers.

Credited with being the first real "boss" of the Buffalo crime "family," Palmeri aligned himself with the Castellammarese Clan, a Mafia group known to have operations in New York City, Philadelphia, Detroit, Chicago and in small towns in Eastern Pennsylvania such as Scranton. Later, when it became Magaddino's crime family, the group used Buffalo, New York as its base but expanded through satellite groups or "crews" throughout upstate New York, including the Rochester and Utica areas and into northwestern Pennsylvania, Youngstown, Ohio and the southern Ontario cities of Niagara Falls, Hamilton and Toronto.

Magaddino's "family" became what law enforcement and the news media found to be one of the most powerful crime families in La Cosa Nostra. Magaddino was an original member of La Cosa Nostra's National Commission set up by 'Lucky" Luciano in 1931 and became a highly respected underworld figure on the East Coast. Magaddino and the other twelve founding fathers of the American Mafia encouraged the formation of families which "free-lanced" crime empires at a regional level, operating with their own commanders and providing the resilience that kept the organization fat and happy for decades.

Law enforcement agencies nationwide were fearing a resurgence of mob activities in the early years of the 21st century as the Islamic terrorist threats consumed most of their attention and government anti-crime spending.

Magaddino began his Western New York crime career as a criminal version of legendary investor Warren Buffett by running a profitable bootlegging business in Western New York which prospered because of its closeness to Canada. He let the Cleveland

Syndicate and the "Big Jewish Navy" of mobster Moe Dalitz smuggle booze from Canada through Buffalo. But in the mid-1930s he had members of the Perrello family of Cleveland gunned down when that Cleveland gang tried to muscle into the Buffalo-to-Canada operations.

Magaddino established long-profitable gambling, loansharking and labor racketeering operations while forming legitimate cover businesses like the Magaddino Memorial Chapel funeral home and the Power City Distributing Company in Niagara Falls and Buffalo's Camellia Linen Supply Company. Much like the fictitious New Jersey "Soprano" family of HBO cable television fame, Magaddino also controlled garbage removal in the Niagara Falls, New York area through a trucking company. One of his waste customers was the coal-burning and much-polluting C.R. Huntley power plant of the Niagara Mohawk Power Company north of Buffalo, New York.

During Prohibition Magaddino even began selling a non-alcoholic mixture he called "Home Juice" door-to-door to the WNY Italian community before associating in the 1930s with brewery owner and soon-to-be Buffalo's taxi king and publicly respected political figure John Charles Montana. Magaddino's son Peter married a niece of Montana's and his daughter married a Montana nephew. Montana, publicly disgraced after he was caught at the infamous Apalachin mob meeting in November 1957, was Magaddino's second-in-command in the 1930s.

John Montana

Though Don Stefano had survived a Brooklyn gang war shooting in the early 1920s, his own sister Arcangela was killed and three of his nieces injured in a 1936 bomb incident. Underworld enemies of Arcangela's husband put the device at the front door of her Niagara Falls, New York home and it went off when she picked it up.

Big Korney, the Polish-American Stefano

During the Roaring 1920s Magaddino was just starting out on his own to become one of the top Mafia dons the United States was ever to see. He and his boys had something of a free-play on bootlegging and other criminal enterprises. Buffalo police and other Western New York law enforcement agencies concentrated on the Wild West-style tactics and antics of a gang of young Polish-American thugs operating out of Buffalo's heavily-Eastern European East Side and led by the blond and good-looking John "Big Korney" Kwiatkowski, aka Kwiatowski. Due to routine American ethnic hatreds of the early part of the 20th Century, the Irish-German-led police in Buffalo targeted the so-called "bad seed" products of Eastern Europe. That gave Magaddino what amounted to a free rein to set up what for decades would prove to be moneymaking operations throughout Western New York and into southern Ontario, Canada and branching out towards Cleveland and northwestern Pennsylvania through alliances with Magaddino relatives.

Big Korney's feats were such that Edwin A. Gorski, one of the Buffalo Police Department's top homicide detectives in the 1960s through the 1970s and a self-described Polish-American historian of the city of his birth, once said that the Big Korney Gang in its heyday was "feared as much as any Italian Mafia gang." The Big Korney Gang's exploits were so newsworthy that they even generated coverage in the New York Times. Though ultimately done-in by a squealer who had been a member of his gang, Big Korney and his gang terrorized Buffalo in the 1920s and committed more headline-grabbing crimes than Magaddino's boys at that time.

Though ultimately foiled by his own perjury after he had actually been acquitted of leading a stickup that cost the life of a Buffalo business executive, Big Korney became a perverse hero to Buffalo youth in the 1920s. For a time in the 1920s Big Korney, seeming to make an attempt to mimic Magaddino's success, operated an illegal brewery in the Buffalo suburb of Depew.

According to Big Korney legends in the early 1920s, one gang member was executed for talking about the gang to police. The body of that disgraced member of the gang, Victor Chojnicki, was found buried in a shallow grave behind a barn at Big Korney's illegal Depew brewery where, police were later told, gang members literally danced on Chojnicki's grave to level the ground and disguise the burial site.

Big Korney's gang of Polish-American bootleggers and bandits—described in newspaper accounts in the late 1920s as a gang of alleged killers and robbers—terrorized the Buffalo area with their killings and stickups until their April 16, 1929 armed attack on the Fedders Radiator Co. plant on Tonawanda Street. During that heist they machine-gunned and killed company paymaster John Perraton in their unsuccessful effort to steal a $6,800 payroll. As police responded to the stickup, the gang members began trading fire with the cops and continued to shoot it out from their getaway car in their unsuccessful attempt to escape.

Big Korney, who had an arrest record Buffalo police described as "being a mile long," including allegations that he had engaged in a revolver fight with rival beer gangs in the Buffalo suburb of Cheektowaga in the mid-1920s, was arrested for the Fedders heist. Despite the published comments of Buffalo's then-Police Commissioner James W. Higgins and the department's detective chief John G. Reville that there was legally sufficient corroboration of Big Korney's personal participation in the fatal Fedders heist, he was eventually acquitted of complicity in that crime. Big Korney's good buddy Stephen "Bolly" Ziolkowski and later-snitch Anthony Kalkiewicz both were sentenced to death for their convictions in the fatal Fedders heist. Only Ziolkowski ultimately died in the electric chair. Kalkiewicz' sentence was commuted to life in prison after he turned states-evidence on Big Korney.

Big Korney was acquitted of the bloody Fedders stickup in October 1929 because 35 witnesses who testified for prosecutors admitted they could not identify him as being at the scene during the Fedders heist. However as part of Big Korney's effort to save the life of "Bolly," he took the stand after his own acquittal and falsely claimed he and Ziolkowski were both in a bar on Buffalo's Sycamore Street during the Fedders holdup. That led to his indictment and conviction on perjury charges and a 20-year prison term.

Big Korney was released in 1940 after serving ten years of that perjury sentence but he was returned to prison after three months of freedom for "activity" that violated terms of his parole. Big Korney's 1940 release from prison, though short-lived, was such big news at the time that the Buffalo Courier-Express newspaper ran that story with a big headline: BIG KORNEY'S PRISON TERM ENDS TUESDAY. After spending a total of 14 years behind bars Big Korney was released in June 1944 at the age of 38. Before he left New York State's Auburn Prison he was told by prison officials that he had to stay at least 100 miles from Buffalo for the rest of his life or be immediately re-imprisoned.

During the former beer peddler's meteoric and relatively short-lived crime career which may have been fostered by the two years he spent in a New York reformatory for his crimes as a juvenile delinquent, Big Korney ultimately was involved in more major crimes in Buffalo during the roaring 1920s, according to contemporary newspaper accounts, than some of the city's so-called public enemies of that time. Throughout the city's East Side in the 1920s, Big Korney became known alternately as a "tough mug" and a free-spending young man who delighted in tossing heavy tips to newsboys and shoeshine boys.

The fatal Fedders robbery was not the only time Big Korney's boys created more work for Buffalo undertakers. Team member Edward Larkman ended up serving a life term for the mid-1920s holdup of the Art Metal Works shop on Buffalo's East Ferry Street during which one worker was killed. While in prison, Big Korney, who apparently went into farming after his release from custody during World War II, agreed to work with Buffalo Children's Court Judge Cecil B. Weiner. In 1932 Big Korney wrote from prison to a 12-year-old Polish-American boy who kept getting into trouble with the law and who would always point to his hero Big Korney as his reason for committing crimes. At the judge's request, the imprisoned Big Korney wrote to the boy who had been modeling his "career" after him. Big Korney told the kid that "Only suckers don't work. Honesty is the best policy . . . that's the way I'm going to play the game when I get out of here." Judge Weiner later told the local media he took the unusual course of action of contacting the imprisoned Big Korney because it seemed appropriate for the boy whose hero-worship of Big Korney "was leading him upon the rocks."

While Big Korney may have ultimately obtained redemption–never confirmed–one of his most dangerous gang members, Peter J. Dombkiewicz, was still violent after several decades in prison. Magaddino lieutenant Frederico "The Wolf" Randaccio learned about Pete when in the mid-1960s at the suggestion of master Buffalo burglars "Brownie" and "The Goose," Dombkiewicz came to see Randaccio seeking permission to stage another armed robbery on what was then mob-territory in Buffalo. Randaccio told associates Dombkiewicz was the only man he ever really grew to personally fear.

In a 1930 trial over a Buffalo jewelry store heist that sent Dombkiewicz and two cohorts, including the 20-year-old Sally Joyce Richards, to prison, Dombkiewicz had managed to sneak a surgeon's scalpel into court during a pretrial proceeding. With that scalpel he managed in the courtroom to slit the throat of the Buffalo jeweler who identified him as the man who stole thousands of dollars worth of his jewelry. After slashing the man, Pete screamed out at him "That's how I treat squealers" before he could be subdued by uniformed court officers. The jeweler only needed to have his throat bandaged at a Buffalo hospital. Dombkiewicz, along with Sally Joyce Richards—who had become known to the local news media as the "Blond Bandit"—and their wealthy crime-for-kicks pal Stanley Przbyl, were all convicted of burglary for the jewelry store heist. That Buffalo case ended up being somewhat fictionalized in a 1950s B-movie called "The Blonde Bandit" starring a forgettable cast including Gerald Mohr and Dorothy Patrick and former silent-movie stars Monte Blue and Eva Novak.

From 1930 until Dombkiewicz finally got out of prison for the last time when he was in his mid-50s in the mid-1960s—months before his meeting with Randaccio—he had periodically been transferred between four New York State prisons statewide due to disciplinary problems he had at three of the prisons, picking fights with other inmates and guards, and he developed a reputation as a generally combative inmate, according to the New York State Archives.

A Real War to End All Wars

During the 1930s so-called Castellammarese War in New York City, Magaddino sided with the forces of Salvatore Maranzano against 'Joe The Boss" Masseria and provided financial aid to the overmatched Maranzano faction. The Maranzano faction included Magaddino's cousin Joe "Joe Bananas" Bonanno and was pitted against the forces of Masseria who commanded "Lucky" Luciano, Vito Genovese, Joe Adonis, Albert Anastasia, Tom Gagliano and Tommy Lucchesi, at least until Luciano arranged for the assassination of Masseria. With Masseria having his

Joseph Bonnano

Luciano-provided Last Supper in a Coney Island restaurant on April 15, 1931, Maranzano was killed in his own Park Avenue office on Sept. 10, 1931.

Some 30 years later, the Magaddinos had a falling out with Bonanno because of his attempted takeover in the early 1960s of Magaddino's holdings in southern Ontario, Canada. The hot-headed Bonnano sparked what became known as the mob's "Banana War" of the mid-1960s by declaring himself the new head of Joe Profaci's New York family after Profaci died of cancer in 1962. Bonanno ignored La Cosa Nostra's Commission when it had invoked its right to resolve the intra-family warfare in New York City. In the midst of the intra-family problems Bonnano had created, he was allegedly kidnapped by Antonino Magaddino in New York City in October 1964 and held hostage by his cousins, the Magaddinos, in a Magaddino compound in Western New York while for six weeks Nino unsuccessfully tried to talk his cousin out of his New York City grab for power.

The Real Teflon Don

Bonanno, who had reputedly put his cousin Stefano Magaddino on a hit list during his New York City battle for control, broke the truce when he then returned to New York City. The "Banana War" effectively ended in 1968 when Bonanno suffered a heart attack and either deliberately moved or was ordered to relocate by The Commission, to Tucson, Arizona.

Several years after the "Banana War" ended, one of Magaddino's cousins paid the price for having helped assassinate three rival henchmen in the Cypress Gardens Restaurant in Queens during the height of the war in 1967. Gaspare Magaddino, 62, was gunned down gangland style on the streets of Brooklyn's Sheepshead Bay section in late April 1970. No one was ever prosecuted for the murder of Gaspare Magaddino, a cousin of both Stefano and Joe "Joe Bananas" Bonanno. But that assassination was widely suspected to have been ordered by Paul Sciacca whose associates had been slain in that Queens bistro in 1967 and who gained and then fairly quickly lost control of Bonanno's former New York City family.

John C. Montana, a widely respected Buffalo businessman whose mob ties to Magaddino were not disclosed until that infamous Apalachin Raid of 1957, was elected to the Buffalo Common Council, that city's lawmaking body in 1928 and re-elected in the 1930s. Ironically, one year before Montana's public disgrace with the Apalachin incident, a Buffalo area civic group named him that city's "Man of the Year." One of 20 Apalachin figures convicted of conspiracy to obstruct justice for the Apalachin meeting—only to have appellate courts quash all 20 convictions—Montana died a disgraced but legally innocent man on March 18, 1964.

Magaddino was the target of a hand grenade that on Nov. 10, 1958 was tossed through a kitchen window of his own Niagara Falls home but failed to explode. That grenade was supposed to be payback by some mob figures angered over his insistence on meeting at Apalachin—from which he and four other mob bigwigs escaped because they had remained in the mansion of his Apalachin underboss Joseph Barbara. Luckily for the Real Teflon Don, the fast-moving State police team that oversaw the Apalachin raid lacked time to get court-approved search warrants which would have allowed them to legally storm the Barbara mansion.

Stefano quieted the complaints about his Apalachin strategy by issuing "assignments" that led to the deaths of several of his biggest mob critics. As Magaddino always did when he approved an "assignment" to have someone killed, he said nothing, but raised his right hand over his head. His henchmen knew that meant the "assignment" had his approval. His Apalachin "critics" were handled that way, quieting the criticism fairly quickly within years of that public embarrassment for the entire mob family nationwide.

The Agueci Assignment

Alberto Agueci became an "assignment" in 1961. Alberto and his brother Vito, seeming legitimate businessmen operating a Toronto, Canada bakery business, were former Sicilian Mafiosi involved in the famed "French Connection" that smuggled heroin from Canada into the U.S. in the 1950s and in the process became key Canadian members of Magaddino's Arm.

The Aguecis were long annoyed with Magaddino's legendary greed and his demand for a big cut of their profits but it wasn't until they were indicted in May 1961 in a big New York drug case that they earned the harsh realities of questioning "The Undertaker's" authority. Magaddino—always reportedly skeptical of Alberto Agueci's ability to honor the Mafia code of silence unto death—refused to put up money for his bail following his New York City jailing in the spring of 1961. That led Alberto to make the fatal mistake of telling the Feds about Mafia doings surrounding Magaddino, an act of betrayal that quickly got back to the Real Teflon Don thanks to widespread Mafia ties to American law enforcement types.

Joe "Joe Cago" Valachi, who later became the most famous of all Mafia turncoats, while in a New York City jail with Alberto in 1961 warned him—prophetically—that he was playing with fire in talking to G-men about Magaddino's heroin business. Alberto's wife got him out of jail in the states in September 1961 by mortgaging their home in the Toronto suburb of Scarborough. He left home on Oct. 8, 1961, reportedly for a meeting with Magaddino, never to be seen alive again. Alberto's rotting corpse was found by hunters in a cornfield near Rochester, New York, east of Buffalo and still part of the Magaddino empire on Nov. 23, 1961. It took an autopsy to confirm the naked remains which were burned to a crisp were those of Alberto Agueci.

For that assignment, Magaddino's hit men had tied Alberto's hands behind his back with barbed wire, broke his ribs, knocked out a number of his teeth and fractured his skull before strangling him. They then burned off both his face and hands and dumped his corpse in the field in the Rochester suburb of Penfield. Police

Vito Genovese

scientists reported that about 30 pounds of Alberto's flesh had been eaten by animals before the hunters stumbled on the remains which had been deliberately left in a farm field where the "message" of his death was sure to be widely reported.

Because of the New York heroin case, Vito Agueci ended up doing time at the Atlanta Federal Penitentiary along with Genovese crime family boss Vito Genovese and Valachi. Wrongly blaming Valachi for having ratted to Magaddino about his brothers' talks with the G-men,

Agueci falsely told Genovese that Valachi had been talking to the Feds about his crime family's operation. That prompted Genovese to order the prison "execution" of Valachi, only to have "Joe Cago" learn of the order and in 1962 mistakenly kill an inmate he had incorrectly thought had been assigned by the imprisoned Don to kill him. After he was sentenced to life in prison for that murder, Valachi ended up spilling his guts about the mob to the U.S. Congress. In the irony of ironies, Valachi ended up being buried in a Niagara Falls, New York, cemetery just miles from the Real Teflon Don's former funeral home.

Magaddino's habit of speaking more with his hands than his mouth when signaling mob jobs made a mockery of the hundreds of thousands of dollars the FBI had spent wire-tapping his Niagara Falls operations and later proved frustrating to the Forest Avenue Boys gifted Sicilian-language interpreter the Italy-born State Trooper Anthony "Tony" Dirienz. After the FBI dumped the Magaddino wires on the Forest Avenue Boys and Dirienz, it was learned that the G-men had planted one bug in what they incorrectly assumed would be a display casket Magaddino and his troops would leave unattended. Tony Dirienz was ultimately to wonder why the Boys even bothered to keep monitoring the FBI Magaddino wires since their own wires were proving so productive. The Boys and Dirienz came to the conclusion that the Real Teflon Don's underlings had found the FBI casket bug and made sure nothing of value was discussed in front of it or at Magaddino's home in Lewiston.

Despite the extensive government inquiries into La Cosa Nostra activities generated by the New York State Police Apalachin raid of November 1957, authorities never could conclusively prove the Real Teflon Don had been hiding in the Barbara mansion during the raid even though his brother, Antonio, his adviser John C. Montana, and his son-in-law James A. LaDuca were all identified as delegates to that convention by police. After a year or so of unsuccessful efforts to force Don Stefano to testify during state probes about the Apalachin meeting, on Election Day November 1958 a state trooper in Lewiston, NY, finally served him with a government subpoena as his black limousine pulled up to his known polling place.

Don Stefano, in addition to being a financial contributor to several Niagara Falls area churches, was known to be so proud of his American citizenship that he never missed a chance to vote. When Don Stefano was finally forced to testify under oath about the Apalachin convention, he invoked his Fifth Amendment right against self-incrimination 37 times, listing his occupation as a salesman for Buffalo's Camellia Linen Supply Co. which was named after his beloved wife.

The Real Teflon Don

Joe Cago

Magaddino's control of the Cosa Nostra's Buffalo-based kingdom that once stretched north as far as Toronto, west to Cleveland, south to Pittsburgh and east to Utica, NY, was publicly confirmed by mob-turncoat Joe Valachi during his testimony before the U.S. Senate Investigations Committee in September 1963. On Valachi's first day on the stand, Sept. 27, 1963, he derisively referred to Magaddino as "Steve"—something Valachi would never do in front of the Real Teflon Don and expect to continue breathing. Valachi told the committee Magaddino's domain extended north to Toronto, Canada then controlled by Vito Agueci, who Valachi referred to as the "grease ball." In referring to the Agueci-Magaddino relationship Valachi told the senate committee "Toronto and Buffalo are one and the same" and Agueci's "with Steve in Buffalo." Valachi made no mention of the fate of Alberto Agueci. Valachi's Washington DC testimony in 1963—at which he identified Magaddino as the mob boss who selected the Apalachin site for the infamous November 1957 mob convention—prompted the news media to camp out at the 72-year-old ailing Magaddino's palatial one-story Lewiston, NY home, every window of which was covered by turquoise drapes.

In September 1963, Valachi bragged before the Senate Investigations committee of having met Magaddino in Buffalo in the 1930s to get money from him. Valachi, speaking kindly about the elderly Western New York mob king, told the Senate panel that in the early 1930s Magaddino had entertained him royally at a time when his own New York City mob associates were dissing him. Valachi told the panel that during a period when there was a short break in the violent warfare that had broken out between Italian-American mobsters of Neapolitan and Sicilian origin, Magaddino had lent him $500 which he never had to repay. He told the Washington solons that the Magaddino "loan" had come at a time when Salvatore Maranzano, then the "boss of all bosses" in New York City had staged a fund-raising drive in New York to replenish the mob's treasury that had been exhausted by the deadly gang intramural fight with donations coming from Al Capone in Chicago and Magaddino on behalf of what he called "the Buffalo mob." Valachi said that, as one of the "soldiers" under Maranzano, he was denied a share of the proceeds of that fund-raising. He said that when he complained later to Maranzano he was told in an off-handed way that he hadn't been paid because Maranzano "didn't want to lose me" as a loyal soldier. Valachi, upset about the suspicion that he would have deserted Maranzano, told the congressmen he went to Buffalo to see Magaddino. He said he "stayed with Steve (Magaddino) for seven or eight days" and Magaddino lent him the $500. "That was about the only income I ever received from my Cosa Nostra connections. At least that's all I recall," Valachi testified.

Under questioning from Sen. John L. McClellan (D-Arkansas), chair of the Senate subcommittee, Valachi corrected a mistaken Washington assumption that Buffalo's two daily newspapers, the Courier-Express and the then-Buffalo Evening News had named John C. Montana the city's "man of the year" in 1956 for his charity efforts. He said a police-linked group publicly honored Montana, then still a key Magaddino underling, for his civic largess. Valachi's testimony before the Senate panel made public a decade-old rift between Magaddino and the by-then-imprisoned New York City boss Vito Genovese, one of those stopped and questioned at the 1957 Apalachin mob convention.

Genovese, who Valachi told the senate panel had tried to have him killed in 1962 at the Federal prison in Atlanta, Ga., for his supposed disloyalty and purported involvement in the prison murder of a Genovese associate, had feuded with Magaddino over Magaddino's selection of Apalachin as the site of the meeting of mob higher ups. The Chicago Sun-Times newspaper in October 1963 disclosed the rift between Genovese and Magaddino as Valachi was testifying in Washington based on what the newspapers described as "the network of informants the government" had "developed within the brotherhood" of the Cosa Nostra-dominated criminal world. The newspapers said Genovese and Magaddino had first fallen out over the 1957 mob public-relations disaster at Apalachin, stressing that since Valachi's Washington testimony had begun, lieutenants of the then-imprisoned Genovese had "spread the word in New York the big boss (the imprisoned Genovese) blames" Valachi's disclosures "on a conspiracy against him by Magaddino." The mob informants, according to the Chicago newspaper, claimed in 1963 that Magaddino, incensed at Genovese's accusations of mob treachery on his part, had told his Cosa Nostra higher up pals that the "uproar" created by Valachi's testimony before the senate panel "never would have occurred if Genovese had not attempted to kill Valachi in Atlanta federal prison" in 1962.

Valachi's senate testimony also confirmed suspicions that Magaddino's Buffalo empire had operated for decades with little or no direct interference by the Western New York police departments or federal or state agencies prior to the launching of the Forest Avenue-based State Police squad which began secretly monitoring its operations in the 1960s. In Valachi's October 1963 senate testimony he disclosed Magaddino's Buffalo-based mob family of between 100 and 125 active members was the largest gangland syndicate of the Cosa Nostra operating outside of New York City and Chicago. Valachi also identified Frederico Randaccio, alias Fred Lupo, alias Freddie The Wolf, as Magaddino's "underboss" of the Buffalo family, having replaced Salvatore Pieri, the brother-in-law of former Buffalo public enemy number one Joe DiCarlo when Pieri got a 10-year federal prison term in Cleveland in a multi-million dollar narcotics smuggling case.

At the Senate hearings in October 1963, Buffalo Police Lt. Michael A. Amico, head of that agency's Criminal Intelligence Division and longtime head of the Buffalo police narcotics squad and a future Erie County sheriff who ultimately gained a national reputation for his fearless public testimony about Cosa Nostra operations in Western New York, confirmed Valachi's claims about the Magaddino command structure. Testimony by Valachi and Amico disclosed that Sal Pieri had been paroled in May 1963 on the federal drug conviction and his brother John Pieri was serving a life sentence for an Ohio murder conviction which led to Randaccio taking over more power under Magaddino and replacing John C. Montana who had successfully pleaded with Magaddino to be demoted after the Apalachin mob disaster of 1957.

The Real Teflon Don

On Oct. 16, 1963 Amico told the Senate panel Magaddino was the "irrefutable lord paramount and titular head of syndicated organized crime in the Buffalo-Niagara Falls-Toronto areas." He made it clear to the senators that Magaddino exercised "absolute control of all illegal operations that pertain to organized criminal activity" in that region and Amico said "no crime by members of the organization is permitted without his (Magaddino's) permission and guidance." Backed at the hearing by Buffalo Police Commissioner William H. Schneider, Det. Sgt. Samuel Giambrone and Buffalo Deputy Corporation Counsel Robert Casey, Amico used a detailed chart showing Magaddino atop an organization in which Montana, Randaccio and Salvatore Pieri and 17 others were listed as his top advisors. Amico told the panel Magaddino underlings were variously arrested for assault, robbery, grand larceny, burglary, gambling, narcotics, murder, extortion and possession of burglary tools. Amico used other charts to show the Magaddino family's "colored ties" to Buffalo area African-American criminals including Marshall Miles, Fred Perry, Leroy Watson and Alver Purks and its "Jewish ties" including Herman Weinstein, Sam Freedman and Sharkey Ehrenreich. He said the Buffalo underworld was all overseen by then-Magaddino underboss Fred Randaccio.

The panel was also told of the Magaddino control of organized narcotics distribution in the Buffalo region under a chain of field commanders Amico identified as "European smugglers" including Albert and Vito Agueci. Amico told the panel the Aguecis passed the contraband onto Canadian suppliers Albert Volpe, Paul Volpe, Daniel Gasbarini, John Papalia, Frank Cipolla and Charles Cipolla who in turn passed the narcotics along to Buffalo smugglers Mike Tascarella, Joseph Augello, Buffalo distributor Carl Merz, Buffalo wholesalers Bernie McCall and Ernie Crockett and through them to street sellers and drug addicts.

Talking about the Magaddino narcotics empire, Amico and Giambrone told the senators that one of the most vicious gangland murders was the mutilation and torture murder of Alberto Agueci. Amico and Giambrone graphically described for the senators how Agueci was ritualistically tortured before he was strangled and doused with gasoline and set on fire. "In effect, his murder was a message to anyone else who had the temerity or gall to assert vengeance against the hierarchy," Amico told the Washington panel, calling Agueci's painful death "a typical gangland murder." Amico agreed with the estimates of Valachi that the Buffalo Cosa Nostra consisted of 100-125 persons, adding that he calculated it operated with 75-80 in Buffalo, more than 20 in Niagara Falls and more than 20 in the Canadian area near Western New York.

Amico also told the senate panel that in late 1963 Magaddino was "still very active in both legitimate and illegitimate businesses" and John C. Montana was still very active in the taxi business around Buffalo. Amico described efforts of the operators of the Magaddino "legitimate businesses" in the Buffalo area to try to intimidate customers into taking services offered in linen supplies, cigarette vending machines and juke boxes. Amico's 1963 testimony also forced Buffalo-based court officials to stop sending jurors at local trials to dine at the Magaddino mob-controlled Peace Bridge Motel at Porter and Lakeview avenues several miles from the downtown courthouses.

For years, deliberating juries had routinely been driven to the Magaddino "diner" and back to the courthouse in taxis operated by the Montana-owned Van Dyke cab company. Amico told the senate panel the Peace Bridge Motel was owned and operated by Magaddino associate Herman Weinstein who he said was believed to have "profited handsomely" from bootlegging, black market gasoline sales during World War II and many other illegitimate transactions." The testimony of Amico who in 1970 become Erie County sheriff—the culmination of his near-legendary career-long fight against mob and drug dealing in Western New York— prompted local court officials to claim they had been unaware of Weinstein's reputation until the disclosures in Washington. Amico's testimony prompted the quick cancellation of a four-year deal Weinstein had worked out for feeding jurors.

Though jurors subsequently were walked to the Buffalo Athletic Club near the downtown courts for lunches, in foul weather they were still driven by Montana company cabs to a hotel outside walking distance for jurors until New York State—shortly after the Valachi hearings—dropped the practice of providing meals for courtroom jurors except during actual jury deliberations.

The Real Teflon Don

The testimony of Amico and the other Buffalo officials prompted panel chair Sen. John McClellan (D-Ark) to say their public disclosures "will help convince the public that something must be done about crime" and that law enforcement agencies confronted by organized criminals like Magaddino and his army of thugs must have "help in dealing with this problem."

New York Sen. Jacob J. Javits said he had some doubts about the propriety and effectiveness of the Valachi hearings until Amico took the stand. "I think the testimony of Lt. Michael A. Amico of the Buffalo Criminal Intelligence Bureau has been a splendid summary of the relation of the various criminal syndicates around the nation into one master syndicate with its top hierarchy of crime and these revelations have been extremely important to the American people," Javits said.

Parenthetically, Stefano Magaddino's hatred of the offspring of Joe Kennedy, who earned millions through rum running during Prohibition, led to him telling his top bosses in the 1960s that he wanted President John F. Kennedy and his brother's Bobby and Teddy killed. Though there is no concrete evidence to link Magaddino to the assassinations of JFK and Bobby, his longtime underboss Fred Randaccio was for a time suspected of playing an active role in trying to arrange those assassinations. After the president's November 1963 death in Dallas, Randaccio was overheard on a Forest Avenue Boys wire sharing a hearty laugh about the death of Joe Kennedy's boy with several of his mob pals. About a month after President Kennedy's assassination, Magaddino himself was overheard on another of the Boys' wires telling associates the assassinated president was a "mad dog" who deserved to die, as though the president's murder was a sign of divine retribution against Joe Kennedy for stiffing his underworld buddies during Prohibition.

Magaddino, like many of La Cosa Nostra chieftains, was known to brag about "triumphs," whether they actually occurred the way he and his henchmen claimed or not. Magaddino's bragging —recorded by the Forest Avenue Boys—about New York State Supreme Court Justice Frank J. Kronenberg and how he "owned" that judge and Erie County Court Judge Burke I. Burke after they issued defense-favorable rulings in crime cases aroused the suspicions of the Forest Avenue Boys but no evidence was ever found linking either judge to Magaddino's corrupt operations. Kronenberg, an Army captain and trial judge advocate and assistant defense counsel during and after World War II, began his judicial career in 1953 when then-NY Gov. Thomas E. Dewey, a real crime fighter, named him a Niagara County, New York judge.

After Burke died unexpectedly at the age of 61 on November 28, 1967, he was eulogized at his funeral by The Right Rev. Lauriston L. Scaife, then bishop of the Western New York Episcopal Diocese for his contributions to society as "a distinguished jurist, a dedicated churchman and a concerned citizen of the community." Frederick M. Marshall, then a fellow Erie County Court judge with Burke and later the chief judge used by The Forest Avenue Boys to get court warrants for their work against the mob, praised Burke for his "scholarly approach and splendid judicial ability." Seems that every time a judge like Kronenberg and Burke would rule in favor of Magaddino's boys on procedural issues in criminal cases, that would always prompt the Real Teflon Don to boast of how he "owned" that judge.

The Forest Avenue Boys heard rumors that the FBI—again with illegal devices—had bugged U.S. District Court Judge John O. Henderson in an unsuccessful effort during the 1960s to embarrass him publicly for his harsh rulings against the FBI in various criminal cases from time to time.

Like Niagara Falls area prosecutors, the Forest Avenue Boys were certain that Niagara Falls, NY, Police Captain George M. Cruickshank was bought off by Magaddino based on Cruickshank's memory "problems" on the witness stand that destroyed several major cases against Magaddino associates in the 1960s. A native of Falkirk, Scotland, Cruickshank, who was 8 when his family moved to Niagara Falls, was a member of that police department for 32 years and retired honorably in 1969. Inducted into the Tuscarora Indian Nation, he died Sept. 11, 1994 at the age of 86.

Danke Schoen

Though Magaddino proved elusive on wiretaps, the Forest Avenue Boys were able to determine fairly early that one of the great loves of his life, other than his sainted wife, Camellia, was gambling both for profit and for fun, especially when the games were fixed. Because of that love, the Don's boys, with Danny "Boots" Sansanese leading the charge, attempted to coax Wayne Newton, the future Mr. Las Vegas then in his mid-20s and an international star because of his recording hit "Danke Schoen" to somehow "front" a gambling casino Magaddino wanted to set up around Buffalo—years before the Seneca Indian Nation legally opened and ran three Western New York gambling centers.

The Forest Avenue Boys wires confirmed that Magaddino wanted to invite Newton—who had Native American bloodlines through both his father and mother—to meet with him about the gambling deal at a restaurant in Niagara Falls during his summertime 1967 appearance at the Melody Fair entertainment center. Aware of Newton's love of horses, Sansanese and others made plans to "fix" a horse race at the Ft. Erie Track in Ft. Erie, Ontario just across the river from Buffalo and "thrill" Newton with a $1,000 winning bet on "Sugar George," even seeing to it that a strong horse that was set for the same race developed a leg problem and had to be scratched from the race. With all the talk about the fixed race the Forest Avenue Boys picked up for over a month before the race, they collectively placed a $125 bet on "Sugar George" only to have that fleabag run out of the money, killing any chance of a Newton-fronted gambling project for Magaddino. Whether Newton was upset at losing on a "sure thing" or he found Magaddino's "associates" a little too unsavory for his own tastes or because he had business back in Vegas, he never crossed the border to dine with the Real Teflon Don and Magaddino's dreams of a casino died.

The greedy Magaddino, never one known to cry in his spilled beer, had to remain "satisfied" in the 1960s with his high profit "Six for Five" loan sharking operations and the gambling dens his boys ran for him, including the one on Rein Road in Cheektowaga that, apparently with the aid of some Cheektowaga police officials, racked up profits most nights of over $160,000 and created Cheektowaga's reputation as "CheektaVegas." The Forest Avenue Boys were convinced of mob-financed corruption in both the Cheektowaga and Buffalo police departments in the 1960s and quite likely for decades earlier. To the Forest Avenue Boys, Cheektowaga, New York was an "open" city in the 1960s just as Utica in the central part of the state was known as a "mob town" during that period.

The closest Magaddino came to an active show business element to his affairs, the Forest Avenue Boys learned, was the prostitutes his operatives provided to a well-known international singing star of the 1960s and 1970s. The Forest Avenue Boys wires confirmed that the singer would be provided a love interest each time he would fly into Western New York or southern Ontario for a gig.

Based on in-person observations, the Forest Avenue Boys concluded there was a good reason why pall-bearers at Magaddino's Niagara Falls funeral home from time to time seemed to be straining extra hard to carry coffins out of the funeral parlor and from churches for burial. On occasion, tucked under the dearly-beloved one's remains was another corpse—the victim of one of Magaddino's many "assignment" killings who would be spending eternity there, unlike the poor souls dumped under the tons of concrete used to build the Niagara Power Authority plants years earlier. Court orders for opening coffins after church services were frowned upon, although it was suggested from time to time by the Forest Avenue Boys and their law enforcement associates.

The Big Korney Gang had kept Buffalo area law enforcement off the backs of the Magaddino crowd in the roaring 1920s and Dombkiewicz, fresh out of state prison in the 1960s, followed the advice he got from Brownie and the Goose and contacted Randaccio.

The once powerfully-built Dombkiewicz had correctly been advised that he needed permission from Magaddino or one of his senior lieutenants to carry out a "job" he was planning in Buffalo, which was clearly "mob" territory. He was also warned by Brownie and The Goose that Magaddino would demand—and get—30 per cent of the bounty of any approved job and would get vengeance on the planners of any unapproved heists in his territory.

In a wiretapped call Randaccio made to Danny "Boots" Sansanese, he described how Dombkiewicz, who had spent decades in prison for his involvement in the Big Korney Gang that had terrorized Buffalo and its Polish East Side neighborhood, had showed him the two loaded guns he said he planned to keep hidden in a dresser drawer after his release from prison in his mid-50s. Randaccio said Dombkiewicz, who was looking to participate in any mob "jobs" he could latch onto, told him he kept the two loaded guns available because "I'm not going to be taken alive" any more.

Sansanese, always ready to hurt anyone who crossed him, was skeptical of Randaccio's expressed fears of the old Polish mobster. Ultimately nothing ever came of Dombkiewicz's request except in its retelling by Randaccio before his own lengthy "vacation" in prison. But the Forest Avenue Boys alerted Hank Williams about the old Polish gangster's vow that if he had ever been the subject of an arrest warrant the team taking him into custody should be aware of the two loaded guns he hid in his bedroom.

Long a power under Magaddino, the 59-year-old Randaccio was arrested in June 1967 for a series of plans to commit bank and armored car robberies. Though none actually took place he ended up getting convicted in November 1967 and getting a 20-year prison term that ended his career as one of the Don's chief men.

In March 1964, the claims of Valachi and Lt. Amico before the U.S. Senate committee in October 1963 about the mutilation murder of Toronto-Buffalo Cosa Nostra operative Alberto Agueci were publicly confirmed by the Ontario, Canada Police Commission. On March 19, 1964 the Ontario Commission said it had independently conferred with Valachi about the 1961 torture murder of Agueci. That session took place in the turncoat-mobster's Washington D.C. jail cell on Nov. 6, 1963, a month after his U.S. Senate testimony.

The three-member police commission said Valachi told them that when he skipped bail in New York City on a narcotics charge in 1960, he connected with Alberto Agueci and John Papalia of

Hamilton, Ont., through New York mob boss Frank Caruso and was told the two Canadian drug traffickers who worked for the Magaddino family were going to arrange to get him to Brazil through a flight out of Toronto. Valachi said he hid out in Buffalo for four days before Magaddino's operatives got him across the border into Vineland, Ontario where he was picked up by Alberto Agueci and his drug trafficking brother Vito Agueci and Papalia and driven to Toronto to Alberto's home. Once there Valachi was told to immediately return to New York City by mob operatives he trusted.

The Ontario Police Commission in March 1964 also confirmed Magaddino's control of prostitution and illegal gambling in Niagara Falls, Ontario.

By late 1963 Magaddino had turned over the operation of the family's Niagara Falls funeral home to his son, Peter and son-in-law James V. DeLuca.

Joe Bananas

In the midst of Joe (Joe Bananas) Bonanno's mob war in New York City, the ever-greedy cousin of Magaddino slipped into Canada illegally to begin a crusade to gain control of the lucrative Toronto-based crime market for projects he sought to personally dominate. His only problem was being arrested in Montreal in June 1964 for providing Canadian immigration officials with misinformation about his past criminal record on his application for a landed immigrant's visa. Bonanno managed to beat the Canadian immigration rap and returned to New York City only to be "kidnapped at gunpoint" on Oct. 21, 1964. According to his longtime lawyer William Power Maloney, he was seized by unknown men who in reality included Nino Magaddino who took him to an upstate cottage for six weeks while Nino tried to cool the intra-family war Joe Bananas had launched.

In May 1965 Magaddino beat a subpoena issued by the federal grand jury in New York City looking into the Bonanno disappearance. Magaddino quickly checked into the Niagara Falls Memorial Hospital for heart problems. His doctor and a court-ordered physician both confirmed his medical condition on May 4,

1965, the day after he was served with a subpoena for that testimony by the U.S. Attorney. But Magaddino's son, Peter A. Magaddino, 48, Buffalo underboss Fred G. Randaccio, 57, Joseph S. Bongiorno, 48, a frequent companion of Magaddino and Niagara Falls vending machine company owner, and reputed Magaddino associate Samuel G. Rangatore, 57, were all put before the federal panel for ultimately useless testimony about Bonanno's "disappearance."

In late November 1965 with Bonanno still "missing" and feared by authorities to be dead, Magaddino was again subpoenaed to appear before the special New York City grand jury looking into Joe Banana's disappearance. Also subpoenaed was Magaddino's neighbor and son-in-law Vincent Scro. Once again Rangatore and five other Niagara Falls area residents associated with Magaddino were also called before that grand jury late in 1965, only to have Magaddino and Rangatore both avoid being questioned because of alleged illness.

Robert M. Morgenthau, then U.S. Attorney for New York and later a long-time New York City District Attorney widely credited with going after international financial crooks largely ignored by federal prosecutors, tried a second time in December 1965 to get Magaddino before the special panel because of confirmed reports Magaddino had been healthy enough to attend a large wedding reception in Huntington Station, Long Island in mid-November 1965 for a daughter of Gaspar DiGregorio, a distant relative of Magaddino. DiGregorio was the man authorities believed had taken over the operation of the missing Bonanno's crime family in New York State's Nassau and Suffolk counties and had been active in Bay Shore, Long island in August 1965 in connection with the sale of a restaurant there.

With Bonanno still "missing" at the end of 1965, the public prosecutor of Palermo, Sicily, the home country to Magaddino and Bonanno, issued an arrest warrant for Joe Bananas and six other Americans on a charge of "association to commit crime" in connection with a massive probe of world-wide narcotics trafficking. In February 1966, Palermo prosecutors contended Bonanno was hiding in Tunis in North Africa and overseeing a massive Sicilian Mafia narcotics network to Western New York under orders of Stefano Magaddino.

Bonanno, after whom Mario Puzo reportedly modeled the "Vito Corleone" character in his Godfather novel, resurfaced in May 1966, some 18 months after he had allegedly been kidnapped in the rain. He surrendered to federal authorities and was charged in a previously sealed federal indictment with obstructing justice by failing to appear before a federal rackets-probing grand jury which had expected to question him extensively on Oct. 21, 1964—the day he disappeared.

The unanticipated "return" of the then 61-year-old Bonanno prompted then U.S. Atty. Robert M. Morgenthau to declare that the Feds "frankly don't know where he has been." Bonanno never revealed his whereabouts and by May 1967 was being described by New York City and federal law enforcement officials as having regained a position of influence and profit in the Mafia family from which he had been ousted at gunpoint about two and a half years earlier.

With the multi-millionaire Bonanno's New York associates allegedly moving toward total victory in their intra-family war in which hundreds of shots were fired but no one killed, he suffered a heart attack in 1968 and retired peacefully to Tucson, Arizona. Briefly jailed there on contempt of court and similar charges and once fined $450, Bonanno was never convicted of a felony offense and died of a heart attack on May 12, 2002 at the age of 97. Before he died he made it clear to all who would listen that he had loathed his "Joe Bananas" moniker all his adult life.

Though Magaddino lived until his own heart went out in 1974, a "dying" Magaddino avoided a mid-1966 subpoena to testify in Rochester, New York before the New York State Investigation Commission about reports of mob activity in Western New York. Three hours after the commission served a subpoena on Magaddino at his palatial Lewiston, NY home on May 3, 1966, he entered Mount St. Mary's Hospital for treatment of his recurring heart problems.

Finally on June 2, 1966, an exasperated Commission Chairman Goodman A. Sarachan said Magaddino would be unlikely to be appearing at any time soon before the gubernatorially-created panel.

He said Don Magaddino's own lawyers had advised the commission that the reputed boss of Cosa Nostra operations in the country was "a dying man." On Sept. 26, 1966 the state crime commission under Sarachan issued a 72-page report accusing Magaddino of approving a bookmaking syndicate in Rochester, New York run by his associate Frank Valenti, like himself a member of the 1957 Apalachin "honor society."

As it had five years earlier in complaining about mob and political corruption undermining the Buffalo police department, the state commission also denounced mob influence in the Rochester Police Department, calling for a "paramount need to keep police functions free of political intervention" and racketeer-led corruption. In Rochester, several detectives linked to mob associates were dropped from the force publicly but later allowed to return to the force to satisfy pension requirements.

In February 1967, the President's Commission on Law Enforcement and Administration of Justice complained openly that Magaddino and other heads of the national Cosa Nostra had built a multi-billion dollar underworld industry that was laundering the proceeds of its illegal operations into legitimate businesses nationwide. Magaddino and his Mafia cohorts were also accused by that presidential commission of corrupting government officials nationwide with the proceeds of lucrative gambling, loansharking, narcotics, vice and labor racketeering.

The commission accused Magaddino and his cohorts of imposing "a considerable degree of corruption" on city governments nationwide but the commission stopped short of identifying trouble spots. That prompted then U.S. Attorney John T. Curtin of Buffalo and Neil J. Welch, agent in charge of the Buffalo FBI office, to publicly acknowledge a lengthy and continuing investigation of the Magaddino family. But both declined to provide any further public comment on that probe.

The President's Commission on Law Enforcement and Administration of Justice in May 1967 identified Buffalo, New York as one of nine cities nationwide with "extensive organized crime problems" thanks to the Magaddino family operations. That presidential commission faulted officials in Buffalo, Flint, Mich., Kansas City, Kansas, Milwaukee, Wis., Mobile, Ala., Nashville,

Tennessee, New Orleans, Oakland, Calif. and Youngstown, Ohio for failing to respond to a survey the commission had sent out to areas where organized crime activity was known or strongly suspected to be flourishing. Nothing ever came of the presidential panel's public complaints.

Based on statements of convicted narcotics smuggler Vito Agueci in June 1967, Magaddino was publicly identified as the head of an international narcotics smuggling ring with tens of millions of dollars in profits operating since 1950 in the U.S., France, Italy, and Canada. Agueci's claims, which in a U. S. court would have been rejected as impermissible hearsay, were made public at a trial that began in Rome, Italy against Agueci, a New York State prisoner since a 1961 narcotics conviction, and 31 other defendants charged in the drug ring. Because of the mandates of the Napoleonic Code that governed Italian courts, that trial had to be temporarily relocated to New York City so the Agueci claims, made in a sworn statement to U.S. law enforcement agencies, could be introduced as evidence at that trial.

By early 1965, through the work of Valachi and the U.S. Senate Permanent Investigations Subcommittee headed by Sen. John L. McClellan, the Cosa Nostra, with the then-73-year-old Magaddino of Lewiston, NY being described as chairman of its ruling national commission of "statesmen," had been shown to have worked its way into the mainstream of American life with stakes in numerous legitimate businesses. By then the mob was draining a conservatively-estimated $8 billion or more out of the U.S. economy annually through its army of at least 5,000 "made men" and as many as 750,000 non-members employed in Mafia businesses or associated with the mob through joint business ventures.

For months in 1968 attorneys for Time Inc. pestered the ailing Magaddino to get him to respond to questioning on the publishing company's ultimately successful effort to quash a $7 million libel suit filed against it by reputed San Jose, California mob boss Joseph Cerrito. Cerrito was a distant relative of Magaddino who was one of those detained for questioning after being found at Joseph Barbara's palatial Apalachin home during the November 1957 State Police raid. The Sicilian-born Cerrito, a prosperous San Jose area car dealer who died of natural causes on Sept. 8, 1978, had sued Time for libel after its Life Magazine publicly identified him in 1968 in a series of articles entitled "The Mob" as the crime boss of San Jose and as successor to the late Onofrio Sciortino as that city's mob king.

Cerrito, who had been briefly taken into custody at the Apalachin raid in 1957, was identified by Life as one of 25 Cosa Nostra bosses. During a September 1968 court-ordered deposition at Mt. St. Mary's Hospital in Lewiston, the ailing Magaddino complained of severe chest pains as he refused to respond to any questions from Time attorneys other than giving his name and home address. Magaddino's personal physician, Dr. Victor L. Pellicano, later told the news media Magaddino suffered a "severe attack of angina pectoris" during that hospital room interrogation and had to be given two nitroglycerin tablets after his color changed and his nails and lips "became blue" under the stress of the session. The unsuccessful Cerrito suit had sought $2 million in compensatory damages and $5 million in punitive damages for his inclusion in the September 1968 Life Magazine articles on Cosa Nostra leaders nationwide.

In an October 11, 1971 ruling, the Ninth Circuit United States Court of Appeals upheld a lower court dismissal of Cerrito's libel suit. The Court noted that under the U.S. Supreme Court's landmark 1964 *New York Times v. Sullivan* decision and its progeny, Cerrito was a "public figure" and had to prove malicious publication. He failed to prove that the Life Magazine piece on him had been done with "actual malice or with knowledge that it was false or with reckless disregard of whether it was false or not."

Actually, in late 1964 Cerrito had been identified by law enforcement sources as having been found meeting at a hotel in Palermo, Sicily with former Bonanno Mob family consigliere Frank Garofalo for what was identified by law enforcement as a likely discussion about the ensuing "Banana War" the family waged with its New York City mob rivals.

In what was described by FBI officials as a "major blow at the heart of organized gambling on the Niagara Frontier," the 77-year-old Magaddino and eight other suspects were charged on Nov. 26, 1968 with international racketeering and conspiracy counts in a roundup coordinated from Washington D. C. personally by FBI Director J. Edgar Hoover. While the Don was in a car being driven by his 69-year-old brother Antonino, federal agents stopped the vehicle in the 2600 block of Ferry Street in Niagara Falls, New York about 3:15 p.m. that day and handed the "lord paramount" of Western New York mobsters a warrant ordering him to return to his palatial Dana Drive home in Lewiston and appear in Federal Court in Buffalo the next day. A skeptical U.S. Attorney Andrew F. Phelan of Buffalo predicted that Magaddino would likely be represented during that scheduled court proceeding by counsel and again claim his history of worsening heart disease made it medically dangerous for him to appear in court. Magaddino did fail to show up as scheduled for arraignment on the charges before U.S. Commissioner[1] Edmund F. Maxwell on the morning of Nov. 27, 1968. That day his lawyer Joseph P. Runfola told court officials he was "physically incapacitated as a result of his serious heart condition." That prompted Phelan to station U.S. marshals outside the Don's palatial home on a 24-hour basis. Magaddino was observed inside the home watching television soap operas.

Meanwhile, Magaddino's son Peter, then 51, remained jailed in Buffalo in the probe in lieu of the $100,000 bail Phelan sought. That high bail was set after FBI agents and New York State Police Bureau of Criminal Investigation agents under the command of Senior Investigator John P. Russell, seized from Peter Magaddino's home on 22nd Street in Niagara Falls $473,134 in cash, two handguns, a sawed-off shotgun, telephones, two police band radios, two bags of rolled coins and 102 sets of dice.

Also seized at Peter Magaddino's home that day were handwritten lists of the names and addresses of various "visitors" found at the Apalachin home of the late Joseph Barbara during the legendary November 1957 State Police raid. That list included Stefano Magaddino's former Buffalo underboss Fred Randaccio who in 1968 was serving time in a federal prison on bank robbery conspiracy charges; Utica, New York mobster Joe Falcone and Gaspar DiGregorio, the Long Island don who assumed control of

---

[1] Commissioners are now called "magistrate judges."

Magaddino's Nassau County, New York, "interests" after the 1964 staged kidnapping of Joseph "Joe Bananas" Bonanno.

Jailed along with Peter Magaddino in the initial days of that crackdown which came as a result of the Forest Avenue Boys' wiretaps on the mob's Buffalo meeting places—but for which the FBI took full public credit—was Benjamin Nicolleti Sr., 56, of Lewiston who the FBI identified as the "capo" or captain of the Magaddino gambling syndicate. Also charged were Patsy Passero, 44, an unemployed Niagara Falls construction worker; Gino Monaco, 45, manager of the Sleepy Time Motel in Niagara Falls; Sam Puglese, 46 of Niagara Falls; Michael A. Farella, 56, a clerk at the Niagara Sundry Shop in Niagara Falls and Augustine "Augie" Rizzo, 34, of North Tonawanda, New York. Also, Louis C. Tavano, 28, a self-employed Lewiston "contractor" and Niagara Falls restaurant licensee who was the brother of both Robert Tavano, then Niagara County, New York, Republican Party chairman and Niagara County government attorney Samuel Tavano. The Feds kept searching for Nicoletti Sr.'s son, Benjamin Nicolleti Jr., 29, whose day job allegedly was as a Niagara Falls house painter.

As was the FBI's typical fashion, FBI Agent Joseph E. Griffin Jr. claimed in a court affidavit that the "FBI" wiretaps had documented interstate and foreign telephone calls generally to "lay off bets" or get "line information" about the gambling operation's willingness to handle specific bets. The Griffin affidavit also advised court officials that "over the last several years Stefano Magaddino has used the Magaddino Memorial Chapel, 1338 Niagara Street, Niagara Falls, as a meeting place for the transaction of business related to illegal bookmaking, gambling and loansharking activities." All that information was actually gathered through the Forest Avenue Boys' wiretaps on the Don's Buffalo operating centers, homes and meeting places.

An affidavit filed in the case by Niagara Falls Police Lt. John E. Belkota identified the elder Nicoletti as "one of the most important figures in bookmaking and gambling operations in Niagara Falls who [was] the operation director for Stefano Magaddino and Peter Magaddino." Another affidavit named Stefano Magaddino as head of the gambling syndicate with Peter Magaddino serving as his father's stand-in and overseer of the operation with Benjamin

Nicoletti Sr. serving as over-all supervisor of the operation and Nicoletti's son Benjamin overseeing the bookmaking activities of Monaco, Passero, Puglese, Farella, Rizzo and Tavano.

By the end of November 1968, even top Ontario, Canada provincial law enforcement officials were publicly acknowledging that Stefano Magaddino of sleepy Lewiston, New York was indeed the overlord of organized crime in the southern half of that sprawling province, including its queen city, Toronto, where Magaddino had associates running matters for him.

The ailing Stefano Magaddino was finally arraigned in his own bedroom on the international racketeering and conspiracy charges on Nov. 29, 1968. The federal government also slapped $3.7 million in income tax liens on him, his son Peter, his 71-year-old brother Antonino "Nino," and his son-in-law James LaDuca and LaDuca's wife, Angeline Magaddino LaDuca. Two physicians including Magaddino's own physician Victor L. Pellicano of Niagara Falls were present during the bedroom arraignment. Though the federal government ultimately dropped efforts to prosecute Magaddino because of his much-chronicled heart problems, Magaddino and nine others linked to his international gambling syndicate were formally indicted by a Federal grand jury in Buffalo on Dec. 4, 1968.

On Dec. 5, 1968 in Buffalo City Court, Nicholas A. Mauro, then 38, and living in the Buffalo suburb of Snyder, NY was described to the media as one of the Magaddino gambling syndicate's biggest Buffalo bookmakers. He was allowed to remain free on a $500 bail bond following his arraignment on possession of bookmaking records. Based on the wiretapping efforts of the Forest Avenue Boys it was soon disclosed that the federal grand jury in Buffalo had begun reviewing the Magaddino gambling syndicate operations in June 1968 as the latest development in an already two-year old probe of the Magaddino-led Cosa Nostra faction. By late 1968, government officials were publicly acknowledging that the probe of the Magaddino "Arm" and its various criminal enterprises was one of the most sustained government campaigns against organized crime anywhere in the United States since the end of the second World War and possibly even as far back as the prohibition era.

The Real Teflon Don

On Dec. 12, 1968 an exasperated Federal Judge John O. Henderson traveled to the ailing Magaddino's palatial Lewiston, New York home and staged a three and a half minute arraignment of Magaddino in Magaddino's own bedroom. With Magaddino's own physician Victor L. Pellicano and an oxygen tank at the bedside, the "ailing" Magaddino—lying flat in bed and keeping his eyes closed—merely nodded affirmations as his own lawyer Joseph P. Runfola entered innocent pleas on his behalf to the grand jury indictment. Henderson ordered Magaddino to remain free on $50,000 previously posted bail. Before leaving Magaddino's bedroom, Judge Henderson asked Magaddino "Do you have any questions at all to ask me as to what's gone on today?" Magaddino merely shook his head and raised both of his hands "faintly," according to a contemporary news account of the unusual bedside arraignment.

Henderson told the local news media he had agreed to go to the ailing Don's home for the arraignment for the purpose of "at least getting the case off the ground." In Henderson's Buffalo courtroom a day before the Magaddino bedside arraignment, Dr. Pellicano and Buffalo Dr. Walter T. Zimdahl who Henderson had examine Magaddino the previous June in another case, both expressed grave doubts that Magaddino could ever appear in court to stand trial. Pellicano told the judge Magaddino is "running out of time as far as the average longevity of a heart patient is concerned." Zimdahl told the judge that based on his own findings and what he called Magaddino's "volatile personality" he was sure that "if he lives another year that's a long time."

During that Dec. 11, 1968 court session, U.S. Attorney Andrew Phelan prompted Magaddino's lawyer Runfola to strenuously object when the prosecutor asked Zimdahl if he thought it was "possible for a man to develop a phony heart history over a period of years if he knew the symptoms" and Zimdahl responded "In a patient that wanted to, yes." When Runfola demanded to know from Zimdahl if in his "professional opinion" Magaddino "has faked his heart condition," Zimdahl responded "no."

By early April 1969, top U.S. Justice Department officials in Washington cited the findings of Buffalo health specialist Dr. Bernard M. Reen who had been hired by the government to review

Magaddino's medical records and his documented history of heart problems since 1960 in opting to sever Magaddino from the ongoing gambling prosecution. In Reen's report to the Justice Department he stated that Magaddino's heart condition was such that "I could not assure his survival should he endure an intense emotional upset" in court.

Amid the ultimately unsuccessful federal government efforts to criminally "nail" the 77-year-old Magaddino, Federal Judge John O. Henderson of Buffalo told federal prosecutors who had been fighting to get Don Stefano to stand trial: "I'm not going to be the executioner of Mr. Magaddino if I'm persuaded bringing him to court would be like pulling the switch." That legal switch was never pulled and Don Stefano died peacefully on July 19, 1974 and never stood trial on the 1968 federal gambling indictment.

In mid-December 1968, the Niagara County, NY, District Attorney's office and the New York State Police Bureau of Criminal Investigation got Niagara County court officials to revoke Magaddino's "business" pistol permit issued in 1947. That was linked to the seizure of a Smith and Wesson revolver and the discovery of Magaddino's long-standing pistol permit during a police search of his house in late November 1968. Magaddino had obtained the pistol permit in 1947 while living in Niagara Falls on Whitney Street and listing his occupation as president of that city's Power City Distributing Co., an alcoholic beverage distributor. Though the State Liquor Authority (SLA) revoked Power City's operating license several years later for 18 violations of state liquor law, Magaddino retained the business-related pistol permit. After the 1968 raid, authorities learned that Magaddino's 1947 pistol permit application had been endorsed in 1947 by the head of the Niagara Falls police department and two Niagara Falls police officers and that on Oct. 19, 1949 Niagara County Judge John S. Marsh, later a Presiding Justice of the Appellate Division, 4th Department, revised Magaddino's pistol permit to a "good until revoked" status rather than one that had to be renewed every three years.

The year 1969 marked Stefano Magaddino's public ascendancy, along with his cousin and former soldier Rosario (Russell) Bufalino as top figures in the nation's organized crime syndicate. That year the Pennsylvania State Crime Commissioner who had spent 21 months compiling a 113-page report on the mob based on information provided by hundreds of lawmen nationwide branded Magaddino the head of one of the mob's 24 "divisions." In that report Bufalino, who had been fending off federal efforts to deport him to his native Sicily for over a decade, was identified by the commissioner as underboss of the powerful Carlo Gambino family of New York City and both he and his cousin Magaddino were tied to Pennsylvania's estimated $2 billion illegal gambling operations.

At the same time U.S. President Richard M. Nixon—later disgraced because of the Watergate scandals—was pressing for increased federal spending and new federal laws to combat what he called the Mafia's "moral and legal subversion" of the country. Nixon centered his complaints on mob gambling operations and the mob's legendary corruption of police and local government officials nationwide. Calling gambling income the mob's lifeline to profits of up to $50 billion annually, Nixon joined the Pennsylvania commission in complaining about the Mafia's 24 "families." By the end of the decade of the 1960s, all the "families" seemed to be more firmly entrenched and secure than ever before.

Thousands of dollars a week had been flowing into Magaddino's pockets for decades from his bookmakers, loan sharks, prostitutes and the illegal dice and card games he oversaw, in addition to the money flowing his way from control of Laborers Local 210 of Buffalo. Nevertheless the still-greedy but ailing Magaddino's control over his family and his authority as the senior member of La Cosa Nostra's ruling national commission began to collapse in the last few years of his life. The breaking point about his known greed and the long-standing suspicions he had been holding back more of the crime family's money than was thought was the 1968 raid on the Niagara Falls home of his son and reputed successor Peter. The police discovery of a suitcase containing about a half-million dollars in denominations of $1 to $1,000 in Peter's home came shortly after Don Stefano had warned his top aides that due to slower business they would not be getting the annual year-end bonuses they had come to expect.

Magaddino's power among the Mafia's hierarchy had prompted the U.S. Justice Department in the mid-1960s to create federal multi-agency "strike forces" designed to crack the armor of the far-flung, multi-tentacled Mafia nationwide, with the first aimed directly at the Magaddino dynasty. Magaddino escaped legally unharmed but that crackdown sent his underboss and one of his heirs-apparent, Frederico Randaccio, to federal prison for 20 years in 1967. Freddy "The Wolf" Randaccio was convicted of plotting two major robberies including a massive Beverly Hills, Calif., jewelry heist. That prison stay left Randaccio a beaten and retired gang member when he got out of prison and his influence in the Magaddino family was minimal after his prison term. Pasquale A. Natarelli, another powerful Magaddino aide, also got a 20-year federal prison term on a robbery-conspiracy charge for the California robberies. During Natarelli's trial, Paul Parness, a mobster-turned-government informant, testified that the West Coast heists never actually took place. Even so, Randaccio and Natarelli ended up broken men.

In April 1970, Federal Judge John O. Henderson of Buffalo denied Randaccio and Natarelli a new trial in that case even though he found that Parness-linked eavesdropping on Randaccio had been illegal under recently-tightened federal laws which were tying one arm of law enforcement behind their backs. The judge noted that no wiretap evidence against Randaccio and Natarelli in the robbery scheme had been used at their trial.

Magaddino, never shy of eager underlings, quickly replaced the imprisoned and brooding Randaccio with former Buffalo hood and mob strong arm Joe Fino whose dramatic ascendency in the Arm began with his first arrests by Buffalo police in 1931 and continued until he was "retired" by the Pieri forces in the Magaddino family in 1974 and spared the fate of his long-time family associate John Camilleri. Camilleri, one of Magaddino's four lieutenants and a labor union activist, testified with immunity from prosecution before a special Erie County, NY, grand jury looking into corruption in the police department in Lackawanna, N. Y. (just south of Buffalo). Lackawanna was a leader in both steel production and mob gambling.

On Sept. 5, 1969—five years before he suffered a "gunshot retirement," Camilleri showed up for his grand jury appearance with one of Magaddino's own top lawyers, Joseph P. Runfola. Though Camilleri did not comment publicly, the Buffalo news media confirmed his sweet-heart testimony by noting no signed waiver of immunity was filed for him in the Erie County Clerk's office in Buffalo. The luckless Camilleri, then 58, was eventually indicted on perjury charges for his testimony before the holdover December 1968 Erie County, NY grand jury probing organized crime's control over gambling in Lackawanna and Buffalo.

He was charged with ten counts of first-degree perjury. But on Nov. 10, 1970 following a non-jury trial before New York State Supreme Court Justice John H. Doerr in Buffalo, Camilleri was found guilty of only misdemeanor perjury. On Nov. 30, 1970 Camilleri was placed on probation for three years. Camilleri was convicted of lying to the grand jury by claiming he had been alone in the suburban Buffalo home of an alleged Cosa Nostra gambling figure. The judge heard testimony from FBI agents that there had been more than ten persons at that home in the Buffalo suburb of West Seneca for discussions about gambling operations on July 7, 1969.

By late 1969, the Magaddino family was challenging and according to many, overcoming the New York City family of his cousin Joe Bonanno for control of mob operations in the Canadian city of Montreal years after his associates had taken control of Toronto, Ontario mob operations, splitting the take there with Magaddino's higher-ups. In May 1970, syndicated national columnist Jack Anderson publicly mocked the U.S. Justice Department in his acclaimed Washington Merry-Go-Round column on its fumbling of the two-year-old and stalled international racketeering case it had publicly launched with much fanfare in 1968 against Don Stefano and nine of his henchmen. Anderson correctly described the destruction of the case by petty politics, poorly prepared government documents filed in the case and bickering among the various federal officials and agencies involved in that racketeering case.

Magaddino was accused in that case of operating a gambling ring between the United States and Canada as a result of a probe which Anderson stressed had been personally ordered in November 1968 by "tough old FBI Director J. Edgar Hoover himself." In a sign of the amateurish manner in which the FBI had conducted electronic surveillance on Magaddino and his associates from 1959 into 1965, Federal Judge Henderson of Buffalo, N.Y., ordered the U.S. Justice Department in May 1970 to turn over to defense attorneys in the Magaddino family racketeering case 76,000 pages of surveillance data. Henderson spared the federal government further embarrassment by refusing to order the FBI to release to the defendants the name of its confidential informant in the case and he upheld the seizure of more than $500,000 in cash from Magaddino during court-approved raids in the case.

The seeming frustration of federal officials in their attack on the Magaddino crime family came to the surface in the summer of 1970 when a Buffalo federal grand jury was empanelled to assist a federal grand jury mob investigation that had been underway for months already in nearby Rochester, NY.

By mid-1970 the federal government was reported to have at least ten times the number of crime-fighting "soldiers" in the field as the 5,000 or so members the Mafia had. Federal anti-mob spending was then known to be close to a half-billion dollars annually and the FBI alone was using 7,000 agents and about 10,000 support personnel working with the U.S. Justice Department's newly-established Organized Crime and Racketeering Section in its Criminal Division. The FBI was also teamed in the crackdown on the Mafia with the federal bureaus of Customs and Narcotics and Dangerous Drugs, Alcohol and Tobacco Tax, the Intelligence Division of the Internal Revenue Service, the federal Office of Labor Management and Welfare, the U.S. Labor Department and the Secret Service.

Nonetheless on July 18, 1970 Federal Judge Henderson of Buffalo ordered the 79-year-old Magaddino's case in the international gambling ring severed from his nine codefendants, including his own son Peter, due to the elderly Don's worsening heart condition.

During a July 1971 court session while the bookmaking case was still alive, FBI eavesdropping records indicated that in January 1965 Stefano Magaddino told "Bennie" Nicoletti that a fellow gambler had better shape up "or he would have his head knocked off." But that wiretap evidence and some 76,000 pages of similar mob conversations the FBI had illegally recorded from 1961 to 1965 without court orders were ultimately quashed.

The Real Teflon Don

In June 1973, the case against Don Stefano, his son, Peter A. Magaddino, Benjamin Nicoletti Sr. and his son Benjamin, Pasquale Passero, Gino F. Monaco, Sam J. Puglese, Michael A. Farella, Louis C. Tavano and Augustine Rizzo Jr. was dismissed. Federal Judge Henderson ruled in June 1973 that those FBI arrests were the products of illegal FBI wiretaps. In May 1974, months after Judge Henderson died, the U.S. Court of Appeals in New York City upheld Henderson's dismissal of the 1968 Magaddino bookmaking-racketeering case. Among the appellate attorneys were Herald Price Fahringer and William B. Mahoney. The court stated:

> "The undisputed evidence adduced at the suppression hearing established that beginning in April 1961, the F.B.I. placed bugs at several locations in the Buffalo area, including the Magaddino Memorial Chapel in Niagara Falls, the Capitol Coffee Shop, also located in Niagara Falls, and the Camellia Linen Supply Company in Buffalo. According to the government, the purpose of this electronic surveillance was to gather intelligence on a feud between the Magaddino and Bonanno families over control of certain illegal activities in Canada and the Western United States. The surveillance, which the government conceded to be illegal, continued until sometime in 1965. In the course of monitoring the bugs the F.B.I. agents overheard conversations engaged in by the Magaddinos and Benjamin Nicoletti, Sr." * * * *
> "Under the circumstances, the district court was well within its discretion in requiring the government to disclose the identity of the informant as well as reports, memoranda, and files related to the surveillance of 1961-1965. *Alderman v. United States*, 394 U.S. at 184. The failure of the government to produce its informant is fatal to its claim that the evidence should not be suppressed."[2]

---

[2] *United States of America v. Stefano Magaddino,* 496 F2d 455 (2nd Cir. 1974).

The Real Teflon Don

Despite the riches Magaddino acquired and passed out to his troops even in his last years on this planet, the Forest Avenue Boys confirmed through their legal wiretap operations that he remained bothered through his life by his inability to get a multi-state car theft and auto parts operation underway. Despite his success in having his troops set up successful business and home invasion burglaries, and arranging for stolen industrial machinery and vehicles to be "bought" in advance by out-of-state and Caribbean and South American buyers and reportedly getting Tony Sisti, the famed Buffalo boxer-artist and art gallery owner to sell stolen paintings for him (something never formally confirmed), Magaddino died still regretting his "lost" stolen car parts operations. The Real Teflon Don, the Forest Avenue Boys learned, also bemoaned his inability to set up a "legit" gambling casino in the Western New York area, something he had also been lusting after for decades before the Seneca Indian Nation, through its multi-million dollar settlement with the U.S. government over "stolen" Indian lands, got into the legitimate casino business in Western New York.

The last years of the Don's life were filled with physical and emotional heartache literally and metaphysically. His weak and damaged heart kept slowly and methodically falling apart and his crime family did so also.

Magaddino's heart problems prevented prosecutors from convicting him of interstate gambling following his widely-publicized November 1968 arrest along with his son Peter. The search of Peter's mansion by the FBI led to the discovery of about half a million dollars cash in his bedroom. The discovery of the cash in Peter Magaddino's mansion coupled with the Don's cutting of the percentage of the family profits he was doling out in the late 1960s to his surviving capos Salvatore "Sam Johns" Pieri and Daniel "Boots" Sansanese, along with the elimination of Christmas bonuses he had doled out for years, prompted splits in the family loyalties and growing complaints about the Don's greed. By the late 1960s his top underlings were well aware his sports books were grossing $20,000 to $30,000 weekly.

The discovery of all the cash seized in Peter Magaddino's bedroom in 1968 and the eagerness of the FBI to broadcast that to the news media was the death knoll for the once imperial regime. Months before the Feds found the suitcase filled with denominations from $1 to $1000 in Pete's shack, the Don had been telling his men he couldn't afford to give them their usual Christmas bonuses that year because of an alleged drop in family revenue. Peter Magaddino even told his wife that year that he couldn't afford to take her on their usual Florida winter vacation that year.

Following the suitcase discovery, the leaders of dissident factions in the Magaddino's crime family met in Rochester, New York late in December 1968. At that Rochester conference were Magaddino capos Sam Pieri, Joseph Fino and Samuel "Sam the Farmer" Frangiamore. They agreed the dying Don should only be allowed to retain control over his Niagara Falls operations involving his once powerful in-laws and son Peter—who had never been considered by the family's higher ups to be a worthy successor to his father in the first place. Fino and his contingent would control Buffalo-based operations and the Valente clan would control the smaller Rochester operations.

Before New Year's Eve 1968, the once powerful Magaddino family had broken into several factions with Magaddino essentially deposed as the commander of the family, even though Mafia's national commission still continued to recognize him as the boss of its Buffalo family until he died.

About four hours after he suffered a massive heart attack in his home on Dana Drive in Lewiston, the Real Teflon Don died on July 19, 1974 at St. Mary's Hospital in that township.

In the early 1960s Magaddino, known to have been one of the founding fathers of the American Mafia, was being identified at Senate hearings in Washington, D. C. as the "indisputable lord paramount" of crime in Buffalo, Niagara Falls and Toronto. In 1970 a U.S. Senate document updating the control of the Mafia at that time identified Don Stefano as one of the six top chieftains in the U.S.

He was survived by his wife, two daughters, Mrs. James LaDuca and Mrs. Vincent Scro and several grandchildren. Another daughter, Mrs. Josephine Montana, had died several years before the Don. Wherever The Don ended up in eternity, he was given a full-blown Mass of Christian Burial in Niagara Fall's St. Joseph's Roman Catholic Church and buried in the St. Joseph Cemetery on Pine Avenue in Niagara Falls with full church pomp and circumstance on July 22, 1974. News reports said a single floral wreath accompanied his plain brown casket in a hearse as it was taken to the church from the Magaddino Memorial Chapel operated by his son, Peter.

Unlike earlier well-attended Mafia funerals, the Magaddino funeral was closed to the public and news media and only about 100 persons, mostly relatives and friends attended the church service. Reporters were denied entrance to the funeral home, the church and the graveyard, including a reporter who arrived at the church several minutes before the funeral motorcade only to be asked by Msgr. Carl J. Fenice, pastor of the church to leave. The good priest told the reporter "this is a private ceremony. I must ask you to leave." Outside the church, onlookers described a short man in a gold sport coat as jostling television cameramen trying to film the casket as it was being moved up the church steps. That man, who claimed to be a friend of Magaddino, told the news crews "This is the same Mass as on Sundays." Someone else told a photographer "get away from here or I'll break your camera."

Years later FBI mouthpieces "boasted" about how none of the surviving members of the Mafia's National Commission came to Magaddino's funeral, suggesting that was a sign of all the respect he had lost because of the Apalachin raid and his falling out with underlings over the discovery in 1968 of all the loot hidden in his son Peter's house. Knowing that law enforcement cameras would be out in force for the Real Teflon Don's funeral, it made no sense for his fellow commissioners to come for the services.

Peter Magaddino remained a loyal member of his father's greatly reduced crime faction until his dad's death which prompted him to remove himself from the crime family's criminal activities totally. Peter Magaddino died on Aug. 16, 1976. Magaddino's crime "family" continued to control rackets in the Buffalo, NY area well into the 1990s. Some believe the former Magaddino underlings "work" later expanded into the new millennium through telemarketing, pump and dump stock scams and internet pornography with the "family" expanding its operations nationwide.

They also set up gambling and loansharking operations in Las Vegas in alliance with members of the Los Angeles crime family, as well as lucrative "straight" businesses like the Todaro Clan's multi-million dollar-a-year La Nova Pizzeria and Wing Company.

4. Hail Britannia

Brainstorming one day after the Boys had set up their new home off Forest Avenue, Rivard remembered how British intelligence during World War II had developed a number of operations against Nazi Germany designed to fool the Germans about upcoming military operations and confuse German citizens through fake public radio and military radio broadcasts. As a member of the French underground during World War II, "Frenchy" Rivard had benefited from the confusion the British counterintelligence efforts caused German military commanders and German intelligence operations, especially Operation Bodyguard which misled the Nazis about the true time and place of the Normandy invasion on D-Day.

Karalus remembered one of the Boys thinking back to having read that George Orwell based the "Ministry of Truth" in his epic novel "1984" on the British wartime deception plans which had included the use of the BBC and both British and German radio broadcasts. Someone on the team remembered reading how Winston Churchill had pressed for and put into play a German language service that reached German U-Boat submarines which were frequently cut off from Germany and whose crews were more likely to accept "rumors" about the war effort as true. That led the Boys to periodically make fake calls to the various Magaddino-linked phone numbers they had acquired.

In late 1965, Bidwell placed a call to Lead Pipe Joe Todaro's family-run La Nova pizzeria in Buffalo and ordered 100 pizzas to be delivered to a specific local Boy Scout troop. When the pizzas all had to be returned as that troop's adult leaders refused to pay for the order, the phone lines in the Boys back room lit up as Joe Todaro Jr. began screaming at his associates in the Arm about the scam. The Boys got a good laugh listening to Joey demanding to know if any of his associates had anything to do with the scam. In the end, a number of new telephone numbers were picked up by the Boys thanks to the ploy and La Nova's procedures for telephone orders were tightened.

In June 1966, Karalus called the mob-connected barber whose shop was across the street from the famed Statler Hotel on Buffalo's Delaware Avenue and began complaining about how the Cleveland Mafia, then run by John Scalish, had been screwed on some recent deals with Magaddino's Arm.

When the barber answered and said "Who's this?" Karalus told him "Tops from Cleveland."

"Who's Tops? I don't know any Tops from Cleveland," came the response.

"Well you will," Karalus angrily responded. "Why did you treat Tommy so bad after the score with the furs?" Karalus demanded.

"What are you talking about," came the reply. "Louis Fummerelli handled that. You got the wrong guy."

"Don't bullshit me!," Karalus yelled back at him. "I'll be there tomorrow and will see you. You're on Delaware across from the hotel, right? I'll see you about 3 and be alone. Your ass is going to have a problem. I got backing from my guys here."

"You're wasting your time," the barber insisted. "I got nothing to do with your job."

The barber quickly hung up and began making calls to Danny Sansanese and other Magaddino strongmen. Camping out in a Statler office the next day, the Forest Avenue Boys watched as about a dozen Magaddino soldiers arrived at the barber's shop about 2 p.m. the next day armed with clubs and baseball bats and police batons, looking for the out-of-staters they were sure were coming to rough up the barber and his associates. The Boys took pictures of all the Magaddino soldiers, including some they had not previously been aware of and sent a trooper across the street to try to hear what they were talking about and take down license plates of their cars for later checks. The Boys broke down laughing about "the war" Magaddino's boys expected to have that afternoon. When the barber closed his shop late that afternoon, Magaddino's men all drove off too.

In mid-November 1965, Karalus called Danny Sansanese about prostitutes. When Sansanese, one of Magaddino's more brutal enforcers, answered the phone Karalus shot back "Hello, who's this?"

"Danny," came the reply.

"Look," Karalus said without identifying himself, "Have a big blonde ready. The one with the big, you know whats."

"Who's this?," Sansanese demanded.

"Me," Karalus said. "I got good money. Get her ready!"

"Do you know who you're talking to!" Sansanese yelled back, angrily.

"I know, the pimp," Karalus said in a condescending tone of voice.

"The pimp!," Sansanese yelled. "I'll kick the shit out of you. This is my house!"

"I don't care," Karalus said in a condescending tone. "Just get her ready and I'll be over in 2 hours."

Sansanese, livid, said "Who's this!!!! You come here and you won't LEAVE ALIVE!"

"So you want a tip? OK," Karalus replied.

"A tip!," the fuming Sansanese yelled. "You don't know who you're talking to!"

Before Karalus slammed down the phone he told Sansanese "Oh," he said in a matter-of-fact tone of voice, "Shut up and get her ready."

The Boys never learned if Sansanese slammed his phone into the wall, but the call brought a lot of laughs back at the Office. But moments after the rude hang-up, Sansanese was making a number of calls to his associates, providing the Boys with a number of phone numbers they hadn't previously been aware of and for which they then hooked up as they continued to expand their secret network.

Kenny Troidl, shortly after joining the Boys, placed a call to another Magaddino enforcer and claiming to a "friend" said he heard a lot of street talk about that guy's daughter having been seduced by one of Magaddino's street soldiers whose name he said he was still trying to confirm. Minutes after Troidl hung up all the back room phones at the Forest Avenue office began lighting up as angry calls were made among a number of the Magaddino family phone numbers the Boys were regularly monitoring and to a number of other lines they soon began monitoring as well thanks to "The Kid's" ploy.

5. The Voice of Sicily

The Forest Avenue operation became very productive very early in the unit's life. Armed with a New York Telephone truck that the telephone company had "lent" the Forest Avenue Boys and one truck the troopers kept in the Albany area, the Boys would periodically "fix" telephone "problems" that were mysteriously and periodically experienced by Magaddino's lieutenants and upper-level soldiers. The Boys also planted live wires and bugs in the restaurants and other public places Magaddino's upper management frequented.

For the most part that worked out beautifully, but the always cautious Magaddino management team would often either begin or only speak in their native or ancestral Sicilian when discussing "assignments," money-making plans and evaluating the information they paid various Western New York law enforcement officials to provide them. The wires also recorded the gangsters periodically cursing the FBI and complaining about who had "betrayed" the Family after one of the Boys information-gathering operations foiled a lucrative "job," either at the proposed scene of the crime or in the "theft" of all the stolen goods afterward.

A New York Telephone truck kept in Western New York was stored by The Boys in a barn in Wyoming County, New York east of Buffalo so it was always ready for the Boys' jobs fixing telephone problems "mysteriously" experienced by Magaddino's legions. Such telephone problems were always "created" by "Red," a good pal of the Boys employed by the telephone company. "Red" would reroute to the Boys' Forest Avenue office trouble calls from the telephones the Boys had indicated they wanted to tap.

Maury Gavin, like the entire team, quickly became frustrated to learn that a lot of the time Magaddino's boys spoke to each other in their native Sicilian. To counter that language problem the Boys got State Police higher ups to assign them a Sicilian-speaking trooper who turned out to be Italian-born Trooper Anthony "Tony" Dirienz. He was sent to Buffalo to work with them at the office translating the Sicilian conversations into plain and tactically-useful English. Dirienz had learned Sicilian when his Tuscany grandmother had sent him to the seminary at age 6 with the hope that he would eventually become a Roman Catholic priest and maybe eventually Pope. Italian grandmothers, like all grandmothers, dream big dreams. Under rigorous seminary rules in the 1930's, students in Italy had to learn several foreign languages. Tony picked Sicilian as one of his. After coming to the United States in the 1940s he was drafted into the U.S. Army and fought in the Korean War. After military service Tony, though he had graduated from an Italian lyceum, went back to school in America and at 24 years of age got an American high school diploma. After a year of studies at LeMoyne College, Tony joined the New York State Police in 1957 as the first Italian immigrant to become a member of the force.

Soon after becoming an on-duty trooper, Tony and Lewis W. Mentis, one of the first African-American members of the State Police, were both assigned to do undercover work in the Buffalo, New York area. That brought Tony to the attention of Gavin and Rivard and he was recruited for the Boys' unit.

Ultimately Dirienz did such a great job translating for the Forest Avenue Boys that Edgar D. Croswell, the famed trooper who put together the 1957 Apalachin Raid that blew the cover off the Mafia, in the 1970s brought him to New York City to work with the State Organized Crime Task Force on a post-French Connection investigation of Corsican and Sicilian narcotics smuggling into the country through the Big Apple.

For Croswell, Tony worked undercover on Ward Island, living in a flea bag hotel in Astoria. That investigation led to the seizure of 110 kilos of heroin and further work for Tony on another New

York City drug investigation of Sicilian drug traffickers. Croswell had Tony interpret telephone calls from Sicily that came into New York City during the early morning hours due to the time differences between the U.S. and Europe.

At age 79 in late 2009 Dirienz, still living in the Syracuse, New York area where he had raised his family and retired from the State Police in 1989, had mixed feelings about what in actuality had been his very important undercover and translation work as a trooper. During a 2009 interview Dirienz, who then had heart problems but vowed to live to 100, said he felt his "loner" disposition and his "maverick" attitude toward law enforcement was the reason he retired only as a BCI investigator rather than as a senior investigator. Being shipped all across the state during his 31-year police career had led his wife to divorce him after 30 years of marriage because he had been away from her and their kids for long periods of time on a number of his assignments.

Though Dirienz thought little of his legendary Sicilian interpretations for the Forest Avenue Boys—something his Central New York family and neighbors never learned about—he had played a key role in the New York State Police war against organized crime. Dirienz died in Liverpool, New York on May 13, 2011 at the age of 81.

6. The FBI Wires

State Police Superintendent Arthur Cornelius Jr., a former FBI agent, agreed to take over the FBI's Magaddino wiretaps in the mid-1960s. That prompted Hank Williams, a gifted tactician and skilled politician who could have made a name for himself in New York State politics had he ever taken that plunge, to belatedly agree to give the FBI access to his skilled Buffalo undercover electronic surveillance team. The Boys grew to distrust the G-men more and more the longer they dealt with them. The back room where the wiretaps and live bugs were monitored was never open to FBI agents who regularly came to leech information from the Boys.

The decision of Cornelius, who was hired by Gov. Rockefeller with a mandate to reorganize and modernize the entire force, and Williams to disclose the Boys' existence to the FBI irked Gavin and other members of the team. But, loyal to the corps, they all soldiered on. Still, only several weeks after the FBI agents began making their nearly daily visits in the late 1960s, Eddie Pawlak got so angry about their cocky attitudes that he came close to throwing one down the stairs leading up to the team's electronic nerve center.

Once the FBI's self-important Joe Griffin got involved in daily trips to the Forest Avenue Boys secret lair, he began asking "friendly" questions about the successful mob wiretapping operation. He even tried—unsuccessfully—to get the telephone numbers being followed by the hardworking State Police team. Little did Griffin and other FBI types know that the team had quickly befriended and quietly paid a female New York Telephone supervisor to deny Griffin and his FBI cronies access to the telephone numbers the state police unit had bugged. Griffin never learned of the inside woman the Forest Avenue Boys had helping them at the phone company.

The Forest Avenue Boys were shocked to realize after the FBI turned over to them the FBI bugs on the home and businesses of Magaddino in the Niagara Falls, NY area, that the G-men had never seemed to get court permission for their operations. The Forest Avenue Boys played by the law books and got the required ex parte orders but Magaddino and his Arm and their high-paid attorneys never learned of the Forest Avenue operation. Despite repeated legal and illegal efforts to track down the origin of the "leaks," the Boys' intelligence efforts routinely provided Hank Williams and his Troop A forces the intel they needed to foil planned mob heists, recover stolen goods and block various other criminal schemes of the Western New York Mafia. The limited review the FBI had allowed the New York State Police of the G-men's own electronic assault on the Magaddino home compound revealed nothing incriminating.

Through the Niagara Falls wires the Boys took over from the FBI, they learned there was a Roman Catholic monsignor working in the Falls who Magaddino really trusted and seemed to use as an adviser but they could never pin down the identity of that priest. Gavin and the other Boys quickly became convinced that Magaddino had somehow learned of the secret federal government eavesdropping efforts and just refrained from discussing his real "business" within hearing distance of suspected federal "snitching" devices around his compound and funeral business.

After taking over the FBI Magaddino wires, Gavin began asking the G-men about their court-approved monitoring and he kept getting told by FBI "spokesmen" that the court documents had been misplaced but were coming for his review. Those "documents" never surfaced. During an interview early in February 2010, Karalus and Ed Palascak, two of the longest surviving of the Boys, explained that the Boys' ex parte orders were always obtained from State Supreme Court Justices Frederick Marshall, John F. Dwyer and Walter J. Mahoney. Those three judges, in Gavin's assessment, were the only Western New York judges who could be fully trusted with the lives and work of the Boys and their colleagues. Under Gavin's direction, the Boys would get one of their three wise judges to sign the needed court orders at the homes of those judges in the Buffalo area.

Those wiretap orders were never filed in court offices in downtown Buffalo where Magaddino's legions or their attorneys could either obtain them under orders of other judges in ongoing criminal cases or have them secretly copied and passed on to them by some money-hungry court worker who could be coaxed into earning some non-taxable money and who probably had a Mafia-style morality anyway.

The Boys always headed back from the homes of the three wise judges to their own hidden kingdom in the bowels of 400 Forest Avenue where they would map out their next "installation" efforts.

The process led to numerous threatening telephone calls between various of Magaddino's senior aides—often threatening to turn gifted stolen property handler Johnny Sacco into a woman in a not-too-hygienic surgical procedure or accusing each other of talking to lawmen about "the family," much to the amusement of the Boys monitoring all their wires 24-7.

Mahoney, a towering political figure for decades locally, statewide and nationally and a former Republican majority leader of the New York State Senate, managed to keep quiet about his role in the electronic dismantling of Magaddino's empire despite the fact that his older brother William B. Mahoney was a nationally-recognized Buffalo-based criminal defense attorney who was periodically called upon by Magaddino's Arm to rescue various of the Don's troops in criminal courtrooms in Western New York.

Justice Mahoney died at the age of 73 on March 1, 1982 while his brother, a legendary courtroom strategist and a court-appointed trustee of Buffalo's multi-million-dollar Statler Foundation, died at the age of 82 on March 19, 1980, never having found out about his baby brother's dealings with the Boys.

Justice Marshall was a major figure in Western New York court history and presided over many of the area's top criminal trials of the second half of the 20th century. Justice Dwyer was a former Erie County, NY, district attorney best remembered for his prosecution in the early 1950s of graft, gambling and conspiracy cases in what became known at that time as the Buffalo pinball-machine scandals. Dwyer was a much admired judge until ill-health forced him to take an early retirement from the bench in December 1968.

7. The FBI and Its Enemies

Though the FBI will never admit it, that agency's men in Western New York were envious of the success of the Forest Avenue Boys. After the failure of FBI wiretaps on Stefano Magaddino, the Boys' wires produced vital information on the internal workings of the Magaddino crime family and set the stage for the federal government's successful campaign to rout the mobsters out of Buffalo Laborers Local 210 decades later. Almost from the start of Joe Griffin and his FBI henchmen's nearly daily visits to their "friends'" secret headquarters, Griffin tried to get friendly with Karalus, attempting unsuccessfully to coax him into bringing his wife and kids to Griffin's home in the Buffalo suburb of Tonawanda for friendly get-togethers. It was clear the FBI was lusting after the kinds of successes the state law enforcement unit achieved—most of which the FBI would falsely take credit for publicly.

In stark contrast to the detailed information about the inner-workings of the Magaddino crime family that the Forest Avenue Boys uncovered, the FBI's efforts to imprison Magaddino—hopefully for the rest of his natural life—ended in public embarrassment as Federal District Judge John O. Henderson, then chief judge of that court's Buffalo-based Western District of New York, on June 12, 1973 quashed 76,000 pages of FBI wiretaps collected in Western New York in the 1960s and in the process dismissed the FBI's 1968 major—and last—criminal case against Magaddino.

On May 2, 1974 the U.S. Second Circuit Court of Appeals in New York City upheld Henderson's decision[3] much to the public embarrassment of the FBI. From April 1961 into 1965, the G-Men had been bugging Magaddino's residential compound in Lewiston, New York just north of Niagara Falls, the Magaddino Memorial Chapel and the Capitol Coffee Shop in Niagara Falls and Magaddino's Camellia Linen Supply Co. in Buffalo, supposedly to gather intelligence on the rumored feud between the Magaddino and Bonanno crime families over control of rackets in Western New York and Canada. What the FBI described as its "brilliant" case against the Magaddino gambling conspiracy—in the words of Jack Anderson in his nationally-syndicated "Washington Merry-Go-Round" column in the spring of 1970—was beginning to fall apart then because of what he described as petty power politics and bickering among various elements of the U.S. Justice Department and in the Buffalo headquarters of H. Kenneth Schroeder Jr., U.S. Attorney for Western New York at that time.

During 1971 court hearings in the case before Federal Judge Henderson, the FBI's Richard R. Walsh and Schroeder were forced by Magaddino attorneys Herald Price Fahringer, Harold Boreanaz and William B. Mahoney to concede the federal government had conducted illegal electronic surveillance against the Magaddino forces from November 1961 through mid-1965, even after the Forest Avenue Boys were in operation and carrying out court-approved surveillance. During a May 1971 Federal Court suppression hearing, defense attorney William B. Mahoney, representing Peter Magaddino, demanded the tapes from which FBI transcripts had been made because the transcripts "are translated from the Sicilian language."

Mahoney's demands forced U.S. Attorney Schroeder to claim during that court session that all the reels of FBI wiretaps conducted from 1959 to 1965 were "destroyed or erased" after surveillance was halted "after 1965" in accordance with what he

---

[3] 496 F.2d 455 (1974).

said were federal procedures calling for the destruction of such evidence "after a reasonable period of time has elapsed."

During a December 1971 court hearing, Schroeder was forced to concede that court orders authorizing those federal tapes of '61-'65 could not be located in government investigative files on the case. In what proved to be prophetic arguments during the December 1971 hearings, Mahoney said "The government had the burden to prove its case was free from taint from this illegal electronic surveillance" and Fahringer argued that "the (government) record literally shrieks of taint and contamination."

After Griffin and his FBI buddies began their visits to the Forest Avenue Boys' headquarters at the psychiatric facility grounds, the Boys quickly learned Griffin and his troops thought Schroeder was "weak" on the FBI's jihad against the Magaddino empire and not trusted fully by the G-men.

The FBI's ultimately unusable wiretaps into the Magaddino empire were found by Tony Dirienz, the Forest Avenue Boys' master Sicilian-language interpreter, to be largely useless anyway. Tony quickly found that the Real Teflon Don didn't seem to do much talking at the FBI-bugged sites, probably because his agents had uncovered the bugs.

But that was not the G-men's last intelligence failing. Even after the fiasco of Sept. 11, 2001 and the destruction of New York's Twin Towers causing the deaths of about 3000, which was largely the fault of the federal government's emasculation of the CIA, the FBI's intelligence failures became tragically evident.

It was disclosed within a week or so of the fatal shootings of 13 at the U.S Army's Ft. Hood on Nov. 5, 2009 by devout Muslim Nidal M. Hasan, an Army major and a psychologist, that the FBI was among the federal agencies that were aware some eleven months earlier that Hasan had been regularly emailing a radical Muslim imam, Anwar al-Awiaki. The imam was then hiding in Yemen where he was exhorting followers like Hasan in the United States, Great Britain and elsewhere to pursue violent jihad against the West.

Even before the FBI's resounding defeat in the Buffalo court in its ill-conceived jihad to try to force Magaddino to die in prison, that agency was even more red-faced publicly over the disclosure in 1971 of what J. Edgar Hoover had started in 1956 as a spy campaign against communist activities in the U.S.—his beloved COINTELPRO (Counter Intelligence Program).

By the time of the vigorous anti-war protests of the Vietnam War era of the 1960s, the Hoover-beloved spy program had morphed into a massive effort in which Hoover ordered his forces to "expose, disrupt, misdirect, discredit or otherwise neutralize" the activities of a wide range of supposedly dissident groups including student, church and veterans' antiwar groups. In addition, the program targeted national liberation organizations like the Black Panthers, the American Indian Movement and civil right groups, in particular the secular saint of the Civil Rights Movement, Martin Luther King, Jr.

Hoover had become a national icon in the 1930s with his wars against bank robbers like John Dillinger, Alvin Karpis, Machine Gun Kelly, Bonnie and Clyde and the like, but his image began to fade with the disclosure of COINTELPRO.

Many harbored suspicions that the FBI kept COINTELPRO going well beyond 1976 when Congress's Church Committee ripped apart FBI and CIA intelligence programs. The program officially had been "closed" in April 1971.

On March 8, 1971 a small left wing "activist" group that called itself the Citizens' Commission to Investigate the FBI, broke into the two-man FBI office in Media, Pennsylvania on a night when many, probably including the two agents assigned to that office, were home or in taverns watching the Muhammad Ali-Joe Frazier fight. In the morning, agents found the office file cabinets almost completely empty. Missing were more than 1,000 classified documents relating to years of systematic FBI wiretapping and the infiltration of "suspect" groups along with the agency's manipulation of the news media designed to try to suppress unacceptable "dissent" nationwide. The clandestine group proceeded to mail various of those FBI files anonymously to a few U.S. newspapers. Almost all of those publications refused to run stories dealing with those legitimate disclosures, allegedly out of editorial fear they would be threatening the lives of agents or informants identified in the documents.

To its credit, The Washington Post broke the first story on the Media, Pa. heist on March 24, 1971 after receiving an envelope containing 14 of the stolen FBI documents. The break-in caused the official public "close" of Hoover's COINTELPRO unit. But elements of it were believed to remain in operation well into the 21st Century. A year after the Media office was vandalized, the War Resisters League publication WIN Magazine published what it billed as "The complete collection of political documents ripped-off from the FBI office in Media, Pa., March 8, 1971." Yippie Leader Abbie Hoffman was publicly identified as having something to do with the "Citizens Commission," but neither he nor anyone else was ever prosecuted for the March 1971 burglary.

Though largely forgotten, the Media, Pa. heist, which came about three months before Daniel Ellsberg's historic leak of the government's so-called Pentagon Papers, resulted in a six-year FBI investigation that generated over 33,000-pages of data. In the end, that FBI jihad failed to generate any prosecutions though it did create another black mark on the Bureau's investigative record.

In 1975, U.S. Senator Philip A. Hart of Michigan, so respected that the Hart Senate Office Building in Washington, D.C., was named in his honor as he lay dying of cancer in 1976, wrote of the FBI in his capacity as a member of the Senate's Select Committee on Intelligence Activities and the Rights of Americans:

> "Over the years we have been warned about the danger of subversive organizations that would threaten our liberties, subvert our system, would encourage its members to take further illegal actions to advance their views, organizations that would incite and promote violence, pitting one American group against another. . . There is an organization that does fit those descriptions, and it is the organization, the leadership of which has been most constant in its warning to us to be on guard against such harm. The (FBI) did all of those things."

The FBI and Its Enemies

In 1976, what was widely described as a major investigation of the secret FBI spy program by the United State Senate's Select Committee to Study Governmental Operations with Respect to Intelligence Activities, the so-called "Church Committee," chaired by Idaho Sen. Frank Church, documented a history of FBI directors using that agency for political repression activities dating back to World War I, including the rounding up of "anarchists and revolutionaries" in the 1920s for deportation and building up through 1976 with the Hoover COINTELPRO scandal.

In its final report, the Church Committee said of Hoover's COINTELPRO: "Many of the techniques used would be intolerable in a democratic society even if all of the targets had been involved in violent activity, but COINTELPRO went far beyond that. . . the Bureau conducted a sophisticated vigilante operation aimed squarely at preventing the exercise of First Amendment rights of speech and association, on the theory that preventing the growth of dangerous groups and the propagation of dangerous ideas would protect the national security and deter violence."

The Church Committee's final report blasted the Hoover-led spy effort:

> "Too many people have been spied upon by too many Government agencies and too much information has been collected. The Government has often undertaken the secret surveillance of citizens on the basis of their political beliefs, even when those beliefs posed no threat of violence or illegal acts on behalf of a hostile foreign power. The Government, operating primarily through secret informants, but also using other intrusive techniques such as wiretaps, microphone "bugs," surreptitious mail opening, and break-ins, has swept in vast amounts of information about the personal lives, views, and associations of American citizens. Investigations of groups deemed potentially dangerous—and even of groups suspected of

associating with potentially dangerous organizations—have continued for decades, despite the fact that those groups did not engage in unlawful activity."

The Church Committee, complaining about a breakdown in the nation's constitutional checks and balances, also stressed that "Intelligence agencies have served the political and personal objectives of presidents and other high officials. While the agencies often committed excesses in response to pressure from high officials in the executive branch and congress, they also occasionally initiated improper activities and then concealed them from officials whom they had a duty to inform." Governmental officials, the Church Committee went on, "including those whose principal duty is to enforce the law—have violated or ignored the law over long periods of time and have advocated and defended their right to break the law," unnerving government intelligence agents at all levels and contributing to the tragedies of Sept. 11, 2001 and beyond.

Many believe Hoover launched COINTELPRO out of his frustration with U.S. Supreme Court rulings limiting the government's power to act overtly against dissident groups. Possibly coordinating with the Hoover-led FBI Jihad against suspected Anti-American types, the New York State Police in the 1960s and 1970s were also rumored, according to the New York Post, to have compiled dossiers on the non-criminal activities of teachers, clergy, journalists, members of the NAACP, artists, politicians and others.

In March 2008, the New York Post reported that the State Police had a secret intelligence unit that had been gathering damaging personal information on state officials. That unit had no connection to the former Forest Avenue Boys and the similar state police units that had zeroed in on Mafia families statewide and which were shut down in the early 1970s thanks to J. Edgar Hoover's heavy-handed use of intelligence gathering nationwide to further his own political, personal and professional ambitions.

In the late 1960s and early 1970s state court judges in Buffalo were openly questioning the Buffalo FBI's anti-crime tactics. In November 1970, Magaddino lieutenant John C. Camilleri was placed on probation by New York State Supreme Court Justice John H. Doerr of Buffalo, in part because of what the judge called the FBI's "strange" attempt to get local probation officers to influence the judge as a result of a decade of peculiar FBI surveillance of Camilleri in his work for Magaddino, none of which ever resulted in any Federal Court prosecutions.

Though Camilleri had been identified before a U.S. Senate subcommittee in the 1960s as one of Magaddino's four lieutenants, the widely-respected Doerr earlier in November 1970 at a non-jury trial dismissed felony perjury charges and found Camilleri guilty of only misdemeanor perjury linked to his testimony before an Erie County, NY grand jury about a 1969 incident linked to a probe of Buffalo-area organized crime gambling activities. As the FBI labored to get Camilleri imprisoned in late 1970 based on its 10 years of useless surveillance of him, Doerr said of the data provided by the G-men for the sentencing recommendation he read on Camilleri:

> "This court frankly never read a report like the one in this case. I talked Saturday with the probation officer who prepared this report and he said the information from the FBI was given to him on a selected basis. It had been gathered over 10 years by the FBI after surveillance of Mr. Camilleri."

The state judge added that he found it "strange that he (Camilleri) has never been prosecuted by the FBI. We are constantly being told that the FBI is the best law enforcement agency in this country, and possibly the world, but the fact that this man has not been apprehended and charged with the alleged act in this (probation) report creates a credibility gap about that agency."

Though the FBI's own wiretapping had been found by the courts to be illegal due to the lack of any court orders that would have sanctioned such efforts, the G-men publicly claimed Hoover had legal authority under the National Security Act of 1947—aimed at American communists and similar alleged subversives—to make use of hidden listening devices against La Cosa Nostra on national security grounds.

After U.S. District Judge Henderson of Buffalo quashed that "theory" in 1973 as he excluded from evidence Magaddino-related wiretap transcripts, it was claimed by an FBI agent in at least one book that those secret efforts had failed only because "the Warren Court (the U.S. Supreme Court)" had improperly held that those hidden microphone efforts "were not legal and could not be used in court." To try to cover the tactical errors by the FBI, its agents claimed publicly through the writings of Griffin and others that Griffin-led FBI teams "would prepare affidavits reflecting their investigations" and take these to New York State Supreme Court Justice John J. Dwyer, a former mob-fighting district attorney of Erie County (Buffalo) who had actually been one of the three judges assisting the Forest Avenue Boys in their efforts. The FBI wrote that "we totally trusted" Dwyer and that its agents would "take the search warrant to the Buffalo Police gambling squad . . . or to the New York State Police" for action.

The FBI even took credit publicly for the information the Forest Avenue Boys had developed about gambling activities linked to Buffalo's Blue Banner Social Club on Prospect Avenue. In Joe Griffin's self-congratulatory "Mob Nemesis" autobiography, he claimed that in July 1965 the U.S. Department of Justice, under orders of President Lyndon Baines Johnson, ordered all FBI microphones targeted at organized crime terminated because one of the FBI operations was targeting an organized crime associate of Johnson's pal Bobby Baker. Baker himself ultimately was convicted of theft, fraud and income tax evasion in 1967 despite the efforts of his famed attorney, Edward Bennett Williams. Baker was found guilty in 1967 of seven counts of theft, fraud and income tax evasion and sentenced to three years in federal prison. He ultimately spent only 16 months behind bars.

While Griffin implied in his memoir that the nation's commander in chief was at least possibly linked to organized crime through Bobby Baker, whenever the Forest Avenue boys asked

Griffin where the court-approved stealth action papers were, he would claim they had been misplaced and he would have to get back to them on that subject. Griffin never did and he went so far as to publicly denigrate the NY State Police's triumphant Apalachin raid as the lucky efforts of small-town investigator Edgar Croswell of the State Police "working with only a handful of local police." In Griffin's "magnum opus" about how he and the FBI broke the back of La Cosa Nostra in Western New York State, he also falsely claimed Croswell's first clue of the mob meeting came when he "couldn't believe his eyes as he stood by watching the flotilla of shiny new cars pass down the road" to Joe Barbara's estate. In reality Croswell's suspicions—much documented in print—were raised while investigating a bad check case at the motel the mob used to house some of Barbara's guests.

The Forest Avenue Boys watched as FBI mob informants like Billy "the Kid" Sciolino and Frankie D'Angelo were publicly gunned down as a "message" to other infidels in the mob after the FBI became disenchanted with their efforts or didn't find them to be of any further use. But Griffin boasted in his memoir about how "developing and operating an organized-crime informant is an extremely dangerous but absolutely essential activity" and how, in order to "fight the Magaddino crime family effectively," the FBI had to "establish a string of informants."

Griffin claimed that in 1965 during court testimony he refused to disclose the identity of mob informants he was using against the Magaddino mob because "their lives would have been over if I gave up their names." He also claimed that "one of the most concrete philosophies in the FBI is that you protect your informants' identities at all costs." The Forest Avenue Boys got a laugh in reading those Griffin claims years after they and Griffin had left the Magaddino wars. The Boys could only think of Billy Sciolino and Frankie D'Angelo, nasty crooks who were ultimately taken off the streets by their own and punished because of their ties to the federal government.

Though Griffin publicly claimed the FBI passed on information to local law enforcement agencies around Buffalo about mob activity, the Forest Avenue Boys routinely watched as the FBI took credit for all the mob-related crime activity the Boys were recording and passing on to other State Police units linked to the Batavia, New York-based State Police Troop A. Among the false FBI Buffalo "success" stories was Griffin's written claim of alleged FBI successes which in reality were really the work of the Forest Avenue Boys. Those included the discovery of the Sacco-led thefts of 60 color television sets from the Joseph Strauss Co. of Buffalo, the plans to ship the stolen sets to a Russell A. Bufalino unit in northern Pennsylvania and the recovery of $100,000 worth of stolen cigarettes that Sacco stored in the same Amsterdam Avenue, Buffalo, location where the Forest Avenue Boys found and "stole" from Sacco a number of furs he had also planned to ship out of the area.

Griffin claimed in his memoir that his alleged Buffalo successes made him "close friends" with Senior Investigator Maurice Gavin of the Forest Avenue Boys and Gavin's "two assistants' George Karalus and Ed Palascak. The only trouble was Griffin referred to his "close friend" Gavin as "Mo," when Gavin was known far and wide as Maury. Griffin also misspelled the last names of Gavin's "two assistants," referring to Karalus as "George Karulus" and Palascak as "Ed Palaschek." Griffin also boasted of being sent by the FBI for Sicilian language training in California before his Buffalo assignment. But it was New York State Trooper Anthony "Tony" Dirienz whose Sicilian fluency helped the Forest Avenue Boys unravel the talk of the Magaddino higher ups.

The seemingly unending efforts by the FBI and Joe Griffin to toot that agency's horn about its anti-mob exploits were openly called into question in 2002 by Lee Coppola, the former and legendary Buffalo News investigative reporter who earned a law degree on the job and went on to become both a celebrated local television reporter and a federal prosecutor before becoming dean of journalism at St. Bonaventure University, one of the nation's top journalism schools.

In a May 19, 2002, Buffalo News review of both Griffin's "Mob Nemesis" and "WITSEC," a book detailing the creation of the Federal Witness Protection Program, Coppola wrote that Griffin's story about fighting the mob in both Buffalo and

Cleveland "suffers from the continual pats on the back Griffin gives to fellow agents and others he worked with during his career." Generally polite about Griffin's crime-fighting claims, Coppola noted in his review what he called "too many factual errors" in Griffin's book which he said makes it unacceptable for use in "historical research" about the Mafia. Coppola's review noted Griffin "spells names wrong," including Stefano Magaddino's brother and street general Antonino who Griffin called "Antonio." Coppola also noted that in Griffin's book he also "gets facts wrong," misplacing the location of Buffalo streets and suburbs and traveling routes on the Interstate 90 Highway.

Coppola chided Griffin in his book for taking "credit with others" for turning Buffalo mobster Pasquale "Paddy" Calabrese who became a mob informant after he robbed the treasurer's office in Buffalo City Hall in 1965 and whose witness protection program exploits were chronicled in James Caan's movie "Hide in Plain Sight." While Griffin wrote about how Calabrese, after his relocation in the program, "has led a very full and happy life with his family," Coppola sarcastically wrote that if that "happy life" for Calabrese included "going through a messy divorce (in the program), having a stepdaughter accuse him of raping her and losing touch with his (own) family," then Stefano Magaddino, who had died in 1974, must still be ruling the Buffalo Mafia in the early 21st Century. In his review of the Griffin book, Coppola also cited Griffin's claim that he personally had helped turn Cleveland mobster Aladena "Jimmy the Weasel" Fratianno into a government witness. Concerning Fratianno, Coppola noted, others had written about "the problems Fratianno presented" to his handlers in the federal witness protection program.

Self-promoting FBI Agent Griffin and his cohorts were frequent visitors to the Forest Avenue Boys secret office on the grounds of the state mental hospital, thanks to Hank Williams' tactical plan to keep his federal cohorts happy by seeming to "share" key data with J. Edgar Hoover's men. It soon became clear to the Forest Avenue Boys that the FBI was frustrated with the courtroom successes of Buffalo attorneys Herald Price Fahringer, Vincent Doyle, Harold Boreanaz and John Condon in the 1960s.

This jelled into a concerted, but ultimately unsuccessful, FBI effort—spearheaded by Griffin—to compromise those mob lawyers through criminal charges in a clumsy and unsuccessful effort to neutralize their regular string of courtroom victories on behalf of Magaddino's underlings.

Vincent Doyle, later a distinguished administrative judge in the state's Buffalo-based eight-county Eighth Judicial District of Western New York, was targeted by the FBI in the late 1960s to be compromised through one of his chief mob clients, Bobbie Bonner, one of Magaddino's gambling overseers. The Forest Avenue Boys learned that Griffin had promised Bonner he would be spared arrest if he could coax Doyle, then one of Western New York's most successful defense attorneys, into a criminally compromising situation in which he could be publicly and professionally ruined. Much to Griffin's chagrin, it never happened. But Griffin's "friends" among the Forest Avenue Boys got a good laugh or two out of his efforts.

"Operation Emerald," a combined federal-state-and local law enforcement crackdown on Western New York organized crime in 1978 was named in honor of attorney Boreanaz. The FBI incorrectly assumed they could use long-time Boreanaz client Thomas G. Gascoyne, one of the most successful of Western New York's stolen property wizards to convince Boreanaz to buy from him what would later be disclosed as a stolen emerald ring. Though Gascoyne, wired for sound and already facing decades in prison if he refused to cooperate, went to visit Boreanaz at his law office atop downtown Buffalo's Brisbane Building in May 1978, he left empty handed because the tactically-brilliant lawyer smelled a rat and told him no thanks for the ring.

The Gascoyne stunt against Boreanaz created a furor in the Western New York legal community with the Bar Association of Erie County, New York, filing an official complaint about the tactics of the U.S. Organized Crime Task Force. As The Buffalo News noted years later in a reprise on Boreanaz as a brilliant criminal defense lawyer, "no criminal charges were ever filed against Boreanaz" as a result of the Operation Emerald prank.

The FBI and Its Enemies

In 1994, Buffalo attorney Robert L. Boreanaz, the son of Harold Boreanaz who had died the year before of cancer, said his father was "infuriated" after learning that "Tommy came wired to his office" to try to get him to buy stolen jewelry. Boreanaz said federal authorities had been out to get his father because in the 1970s his father had a record of 11 straight victories in Buffalo Federal Tax Court and the U.S. District Court in Buffalo in criminal cases.

Gascoyne, a Buffalo burglar, arsonist, insurance-fraud artist and stolen-property fence with ties to organized crime for over 40 years, "retired" from crime in December 1978 as he was placed in the Federal Witness Protection Program and his FBI pals helped him move to Chesapeake, Virginia. There, under a new name, he masqueraded publicly as a home-repair contractor—actually getting injured in a job that forced him to wear a back brace and left him physically unable to do manual labor. Always the criminal, Tommy, for reasons best known to himself, shot himself in the stomach when the FBI was forced to arrest him in Chesapeake in 1985 because of his activities with a burglary ring there.

Relocated back to the Buffalo area, Tommy ended up getting convicted on Dec. 7, 1994 by a Buffalo jury of burglarizing a home in the Buffalo suburb of Tonawanda. The then-69-year-old Gascoyne, who had fathered 10 children by three wives, always bragged about how he had to teach Magaddino family members how to safely commit crimes and fence stolen property. He insisted the State Supreme Court jury which convicted him of the Tonawanda crime had been railroaded into a verdict by prosecutors.

"I've got too much money to do stuff like this. I'm innocent," Gascoyne told a Buffalo News reporter following the 1994 jury verdict. "I wasn't tried for this case. I was tried for what I did in the past." After an unsuccessful appeal, Gascoyne, then 70, was taken into custody Nov. 27, 1995 to begin serving the two to six year prison term New York State Supreme Court Justice Penny M. Wolfgang had imposed for the Tonawanda house job. Gascoyne, imprisoned under a government-provided fake name, was released after more than two years behind bars.

But the 1978 Operation Emerald sting, based on Gascoyne's months of undercover efforts, had proven to be a law enforcement success despite the fiasco with attorney Boreanaz. The Emerald sting which utilized tactics employed by the Forest Avenue boys years earlier, among other law enforcement efforts, led to 181 convictions and the solving of crimes that had cost victims $7 million. The success of Operation Emerald stemmed in large part from the intelligence collected about Buffalo area organized crime ring activity by the Forest Avenue Boys less than a decade earlier.

Because of the FBI information-sharing deal agreed to by New York State Police higher ups in the 1960s, the FBI learned through the Forest Avenue Boys of attorney Herald Price Fahringer telephoning Sam Pieri at Santasiero's Restaurant on Niagara Street in Buffalo about his plans to move his legal business from one of Buffalo's most renowned law firms, then called Lipsitz, Green, Fahringer, Roll, Salisbury & Cambria to New York City in the mid-1970s. The Boys listened as Fahringer told Pieri he should spread the word among his New York pals that Fahringer was there to deal with them. The FBI had long hated Fahringer whose priestly demeanor had been refined as he paid his way through law school as a television commercial actor. After he moved his practice to Manhattan, the New York Times described the telegenic Fahringer's "blindingly white hair" and his perennial deep blue Paul Stuart suit, starched white shirt and custom-made, plain-toed loafers.

Learning of Fahringer's call to Pieri, the FBI set out on what proved to be its ultimately-unsuccessful effort to lure Fahringer to one of the mob's palatial estates in Saugerties, New York and have him arrested on stolen property possession or similar charges. That scheme was designed to involve federal officials quickly informing the news media of the arrest of Fahringer, a self-described workaholic who did not drink or smoke or eat sweets. Fahringer, still practicing and remaining a thorn in the side of the FBI well into his 80s, by the final decades of the 20th Century had become a nationally-recognized trial and appellate lawyer. He was described in the September 2009 Bulletin publication of the Bar Association of

Erie County in Buffalo as "one of the leading trial and appellate criminal lawyers in the United States."

Fahringer told The New York Times in November 1996 that despite his patrician demeanor he was "just not comfortable in social situations and I have an awful time talking about anything other than the law." Also in 1996 Al Goldstein, the publisher of Screw magazine and one of Fahringer's attention-grabbing clientele such as Hustler publisher Larry Flynt, Claus von Bulow, Jean Harris and convicted former CIA agent Edwin Wilson, said of Fahringer: "You don't use a four-letter word around Harold. Being with him is like watching a documentary about a Victorian-era lawyer."

In 1996, as Fahringer was defending New York's adult-entertainment industry against new zoning rules that ultimately transformed the Times Square area into a tourist mecca, Norman Siegel, then executive director of the New York Civil Liberties Union called the native of the rough-and-tumble coal-belt town of Williamsport, Pa. "An attorney straight out of central casting." But Siegel, inadvertently echoing the reasons the FBI had sought to trap Fahringer, also told The Times that "despite his flamboyance and courtroom showmanship, Herald is not just a suit. He cares passionately about the First Amendment." The FBI always regretted its failure to trap Fahringer though the agency is unlikely to ever publicly acknowledge that fact.

Paul J. Cambria, the Buffalo law firm partner Fahringer had long relied upon because of Cambria's own tactical brilliance, for years was the main lawyer for porn publisher Flynt as well as Buffalo Laborers Local 210 in its battles against the FBI. After its failed efforts to criminally embarrass and destroy Fahringer, Harold Boreanaz and other Buffalo lawyers who made mincemeat of many of the FBI's Mafia cases in the 1960s and 1970s, the bureau made no effort to legally "knee-cap" Cambria, who Larry Flynt in 2009 told The Buffalo News was then "the best First Amendment lawyer in the United States." Flynt kept Cambria on retainer for decades even as Cambria split his legal practice between his Buffalo law firm headquarters and Los Angeles, Calif. where he became a motorcycle buddy of both actor-turned-California governor Arnold Schwarzenegger and acclaimed comic Jay Leno. It was through

144

Cambria that Leno fell in love with Buffalo chicken wings and the pizzas churned out by Buffalo's famed La Nova Pizzeria firm formed by "Lead Pipe Joe" Todaro and run for generations by his family.

FBI Informants

The FBI let William "Billie the Kid" Sciolino and Frank D'Angelo hang out to dry once it became apparent their work as FBI mob informants wasn't paying off in the 1970s. The Forest Avenue Boys found this to be a regular and disturbing pattern with FBI operations in the Buffalo area. FBI mob informants had a way of being abandoned by their FBI controllers and denied access to the Federal Witness Protection Program which had been formed in 1970 under the Federal Organized Crime Control Act of 1970. That national crime-fighting law was radically altered because of the herculean efforts of a young Buffalo, New York attorney who was later to become a federal prosecutor and New York State trial and appellate judge, Salvatore R. Martoche.

Martoche represented Tom Leonhard, a divorced Buffalo blue-collar worker who found that his children had disappeared along with his ex-wife because her new husband, Buffalo mobster and general hoodlum Pasquale "Paddy" Calabrese, had been given a new identity as the first Mafia snitch admitted to the federal witness relocation program set up by the U.S. Justice Department. The valiant efforts of Martoche, a former Buffalo public defender, to help Leonhard try to regain his sons and daughter were chronicled in both a book and the James Caan movie entitled "Hide In Plain Sight" which was filmed in Buffalo in 1978. Though Martoche's efforts ended with Leonhard being reunited with his children in 1975, the U.S. Supreme Court in April 1981 upheld a lower court decision dismissing Leonhard's $10.5 million suit against the federal government over the "Hide in Plain Sight" saga.

The suit which was filed in Federal Court in Buffalo in July 1978 accused the federal government's witness protection program of depriving Leonhard of the right to raise his three children, or at least participate in their upbringing. The suit also alleged the three

Leonhard children suffered "extreme mental, physical and emotional distress" while living with their ex-Mafiosi stepfather.

In 1982 Martoche was named the Buffalo-based U.S. Attorney for Western New York, becoming close friends in the process with Rudy Giuliani who in the 1980s was a U.S. prosecutor in New York City and came to be called America's Mayor over the 9-11 Twin Towers tragedy. From 1986 to 1988 Martoche was President Reagan's assistant secretary of labor (enforcement) and from 1988 to 1990 was an assistant secretary of the treasury under both Reagan and President George H.W. Bush. Nationally credited with forcing reforms in the Federal Witness Protection Program in his work for Tom Leonhard, Martoche was elected a New York State Supreme Court justice in 1999 and on May 3, 2004 was appointed to the Appellate Division, Fourth Department of State Supreme Court in Rochester, NY, by then New York Governor George Pataki.

The testimony of Calabrese, who died of a massive heart attack in 2005 at the age of 66, had put Magaddino lieutenant and former Buffalo mob boss Frederico Randaccio in prison for 20 years on a conspiracy conviction. After going undercover in the federal program, Calabrese lived in Reno, Nevada for five years working as a security consultant for gambling casinos and freelanced as an undercover agent in Buffalo and in Alaska in the 1970s where he played a leading role in uncovering a vice and gambling ring on the Alaska pipeline project. The former Buffalo mobster Calabrese also worked with U.S. and Canadian authorities by infiltrating a counterfeiting ring resulting in the arrest of six Mafiosi and the seizure of $1.2 million in phony money in Vancouver, British Columbia, Spokane and Toronto in a case that was chronicled in a Canadian Broadcasting Corporation documentary called "Connection."

After Calabrese's death in his new home in Kalispell, Montana on Oct. 13, 2005, Lee Coppola, the former Buffalo News investigative reporter who by 2005 was dean of the Russell J. Jandoli School of Journalism and Mass Communication at St. Bonaventure University said of "Paddy":

"When he broke the Mafia's code of silence, he started a snowball effect that led to other informants, other convictions and eventually to the death of the Buffalo Mafia. His life in hiding was the precursor to what we know today as the Witness Security Program. Only, back then, there was no program and no security and Paddy relied on his street smarts and wiliness to stay alive when others wanted him dead. In the scheme of things, the Buffalo community owes him a debt of gratitude."

On the other hand, William "Billie The Kid" Sciolino, 40, had worked his way up into the ranks of Magaddino soldiers. He had risen to the point where in the 1960s he had been making all the silencers the Real Teflon Don's forces used on their handguns and was himself one of the Don's hit men. But Billie was gunned down by two masked men in broad daylight at an NFTA construction site at Main and Ferry streets on March 7, 1980 after he was let loose by his G-men protectors. Frankie D'Angelo, a 31-year-old burglar and jewelry thief was walking to his car with his girlfriend after leaving the then popular Mulligan's nightclub at 1669 Hertel Avenue about 2:45 a.m. on October 5, 1974, when he was iced by three masked men who ran out of nearby bushes. As he pushed his girlfriend out of the way, he was shot four times. No evidence was ever recovered in the clean Sciolino hit. But just 12 hours after D'Angelo's assassination, a teenage fisherman led police to the State Barge Canal in the nearby City of Tonawanda where the D'Angelo murder weapons, a shotgun and two handguns and ski masks used by his killers were recovered in about three feet of water. D'Angelo's killers were suspected of having been gunmen the Real Teflon Don and his boys brought into the Buffalo area. During an October 1990 federal court hearing, U.S. Attorney Dennis C. Vacco confirmed that John C. Sacco Jr., while he was a full-fledged federal informant on his former Mafia buddies, had told the FBI Sciolino had been clipped because "he was a rat for the FBI."

Another betrayed FBI informant in the Buffalo area was Anita DeLuca DiGiulio Marvin. Natively intelligent and a high school graduate, the attractive Anita married for the first time at 19 to 58-year-old Anthony J. O'Hara, her boss in a Western New York vacuum cleaner business. The father of her first two daughters, O'Hara, who moved his family and business to Toronto, died in 1971 and months later Anita married Fred Celani, the father of her third daughter. Celani ultimately served a prison term as a con artist who had touted a fictitious $100 million Buffalo, New York, waterfront office building. Anita divorced Celani in 1976.

Married five times to four men, she fell in love with a fifth man she lusted after and yearned to marry while both were behind bars. Always unlucky in love, Anita, Western New York's Notorious Black Widow, died in prison long after she was abandoned by her old FBI buddies.

Anita had allegedly arranged for the 1985 insurance-money murder of one of her hubbies, former national celebrity body guard Robert DiGiulio and had been a paid FBI informant in the 1970s and 1980s until the G-men abandoned her after she was indicted in 1990 for spousal murder. The voluptuous former Anita DeLuca grew up in North Tonawanda, NY, in the Magaddino-controlled Niagara County. One of her uncles for a time was even that town's police chief. That didn't stop Anita's ultimately fatal trip to the wild side and the FBI.

At an unusual murder trial before New York State Supreme Court Justice Frederick M. Marshall and a Buffalo jury in January 1991, Anita's fate was decided by the judge while the jury simultaneously considered the evidence against her co-defendant, the already-imprisoned mob hit man Luciano "Dilly" Spataro. Testifying in her own defense at her murder trial on Jan. 11, 1991, the former model insisted that, months before DiGiulio was murdered, she and her husband contacted her FBI associates to talk about the fears that her husband would be killed because of his "mob-related" money problems.

Anita testified that after she and DiGiulio married in Las Vegas on Nov. 3, 1984, she had lent him $12,000 because his wealthy restaurant-owning relatives in the Buffalo area had refused to help him financially. She also claimed on the witness stand that DiGiulio had trouble adjusting to family life in her home which included her three teen-aged daughters, by two of her husbands, and her 8-year-old son whose father was ex-Magaddino soldier Vincent "Jimmy" Caci.

Caci, who died in August 2011 at age 86, was known as one of the toughest mob figures to ever emerge from the Buffalo underworld. By the 1990's, Caci was a major figure in the Los Angeles Mafia and a wealthy and elderly Palm Springs, California restaurant owner. Caci, in the mid-1980s was still an active mobster on the West Coast. He had been advised by friends that DiGiulio was rough with Anita's son—Caci's heir—and had made the boy, then 8, cry by squeezing his head during a December 1984 family dispute. Anita claimed on the witness stand that DiGiulio, who weighed about 300 pounds at his death would periodically become "violent" and throw things around their house.

But in one of the many prosecutorial coup-de-graces that led to her conviction, Anita confirmed on the stand that about two months before DiGiulio's murder she got him to agree to take out a $100,000 life insurance policy with her as his beneficiary. She was also forced to admit she had quietly obtained another $50,000 life insurance policy on him without telling him. Ultimately Anita collected $115,000 on those policies and got $10,000 from heavyweight boxing champion Larry Holmes, a former client and good friend of her slain husband for his burial. But, she later claimed, she ended up penniless after remarrying George Marvin, a Western New York car and insurance salesman, after DiGiulio's assassination.

DiGiulio, who had began his bodyguard career in Western New York in the 1970s providing security for touring personalities such as Frank Sinatra, Elvis Presley, the Rolling Stones and national political figures, is believed to have become an FBI informant after moving to Las Vegas and becoming a part-time nightclub bouncer and bodyguard to both singer Robert Goulet and heavyweight boxing champion Larry Holmes prior to his marriage to Anita. During the 1991 murder trial it was disclosed that "Dilly" Spataro had planned initially to kill DiGiulio for Anita on April 15, 1985 or April 16, 1985 near a posh restaurant on Buffalo's Delaware Avenue, only to be deterred by a large concentration of police and passers-by. Mob-turncoat Billy Koopman testified at the murder trial that one of Anita's teenage daughters told him that Anita wanted DiGiulio dead by April 16, 1985. Koopman told the jury he, Spataro and their crime pals William "Cookie" Giglia and Giglia's wife Margaret "Peggy" Giglia drove to the DiGiulio home on Fairgreen Drive about 1:30 a.m. April 17, 1985. Koopman testified that "Dilly" waited in the backyard for the DiGiulios to arrive home about 2 a.m. Koopman testified that with Anita nearby "Dilly ran up and shot" DiGiulio once in the back of the neck as Anita screamed loudly for effect. Koopman testified that the murder team drove back to Buffalo, rendezvousing at a Niagara Street bar after "Dilly" had thrown the .22-caliber murder weapon into the Niagara River off the New York State Thruway.

Prosecutors contended that Anita had agreed to pay "Dilly" $66,000 from the widow insurance benefits she received three weeks after DiGiulio's death. Koopman, however, told the murder trial jury "Dilly" was angry because Anita had only paid him $1,200 up-front and dawdled about paying him another $2,500, even though "Dilly" knew about the $10,000 Holmes gift to the "grieving" widow. Koopman also testified that he personally had been promised as much as $10,000 for buying the handgun murder weapon "Dilly" used and for serving as a lookout during the assassination. He claimed he only ended up with $100 for his role in the spousal murder.

A week after her Jan. 16, 1991 murder conviction, Anita spoke to the Buffalo news media and claimed FBI agents Joseph Coyne and Glen Reukauf knew of her previous work as an FBI informant in Western New York and had re-recruited her in 1983 to develop information about her then-boss, Jack Liffiton, an Amherst, NY home builder who the FBI and federal prosecutors ultimately got convicted of fraud.

The convicted murderess claimed that about a month before DiGiulio's murder, she and DiGiulio had gone to Coyne and Reukauf about their fears that "Jimmy" Caci (really Vincent Dominic), by then a captain in the Los Angeles Mafia family, or other mob figures were gunning for him.

The FBI and Its Enemies

At Anita's trial, her FBI ties were grudgingly confirmed by prosecutors on Jan. 15, 1991. Attorneys for Anita and Spataro unsuccessfully urged the judge to make prosecutors call FBI agents to the stand to testify about Anita and her late hubby's FBI connections. But after the judge rejected that defense ploy, then-First Assistant Erie County, DA Frank J. Clark confirmed to the judge that some of Anita's claims about her and her late husband's ties to the FBI were true.

Refusing to publicly disclose what the FBI had confirmed about the couple's links to the G-men, Clark—later Erie County District Attorney himself—offered to let Anita and "Dilly's" attorneys talk to FBI agents in the courtroom hallway and subpoena them as defense witnesses, if they chose. In court, Clark told the judge that FBI agents who had dealt with the DiGiulios "would corroborate" Anita's claims "in some respects and they would refute her in some respects." Clark, saying nothing more specific about Anita's informant claims, told the judge prosecutors at the murder trial would not be attempting to rebut Anita's claims that her late husband had also been a government informant and that he had told the FBI that some of his former mob associates were going to kill him. Clark cryptically told the murder trial judge the FBI had told him "there are some things they could not tell me" about the relationships of Anita and her late husband to the FBI.

On Jan. 16, 1991 the jury found "Dilly" guilty and the judge found Anita guilty. At their Feb. 20, 1991 sentencings, Anita and "Dilly" both got life terms and their lawyers denounced their "low-life" chief accusers in the spousal murder, mob-turncoat and former Buffalo garbage collector William "Billie" Koopman and William "Cookie" Giglia and his wife Margaret "Peggy" Giglia. Anita, who had been free until her conviction the previous month, also told the judge she still could not believe she had been found guilty. "I came before this court an innocent person and I believed in the system," she told Marshall. "I'm still an innocent person. I can't believe I'm being sentenced today," she told the stone-faced judge.

"Dilly" told the judge he and Anita were victims of a "frame-up" by Koopman who was about to be admitted to the Federal Witness Protection Program. A week earlier Koopman had received the minimum-allowable 5 to 15 year term from Marshall for helping "Dilly" kill "Dilly's" son-in-law John Pinelli in 1996.

With the Gulf War then raging against Saddam Hussein's Iraq, "Dilly" told the judge he should have sentenced his former crime associate Koopman to frontline duty in the Middle East shootout. "You should have sentenced him to the Gulf, the front lines," "Dilly" told the judge of Koopman. "He's a murderer, a killer."

In May 1991, Anita's oldest daughter, Michele Marvin Klapp, then 21, pleaded guilty to perjury for her testimony in the investigation of DiGiulio's slaying. Michele admitted she lied under oath in testifying at her mother's murder trial on May 14, 1991. She had falsely told the jury that Margaret "Peggy" Giglia had confessed to the murder. Peggy Giglia had driven Dilly from the murder scene and later worked out a plea deal with prosecutors as had Koopman and her husband.

On June 26, 1991 State Supreme Court Justice Julian F. Kubiniec of Buffalo placed Michele on probation for three years, telling her "I hope in the future you're going to take something like telling the truth under oath more seriously." "Cookie" and "Peggy" Giglia, both members of the Magaddino-run Laborers Local 210 of Buffalo, received immunity from prosecution for their roles in driving Koopman and "Dilly" to the DiGiulio murder scene and acting as lookouts. The Giglias also helped prosecutors obtain the indictment of "Dilly" in mid-1991 for the slayings in 1981 of Buffalo restaurant manager Robert Warner and the 1984 murder of Buffalo mobster Alfred T. Monaco.

In September 1984, Koopman, described by then-Erie County, New York, District Attorney Kevin M. Dillon as the "most productive informant" Buffalo-area law enforcement ever got to work for them, was granted an early release from a federal prison in the state of Arizona where he had been housed to serve the prison term he received for his manslaughter plea in the John Pinelli killing in Western New York.

Anita was still fighting her conviction four years after her trial when the jailed but still-hormone-driven vixen tried to get hitched a sixth time to Forrest Dwayne Miles, an African-American killer who would have been her fifth husband.

On April 21, 1995, Miles was sentenced by New York State Supreme Court Justice Mario J. Rossetti to 37 and one-half years to life for the March 1993 murder of a man in a Buffalo deli stickup and the May 1993 murder of a 15-year-old Buffalo boy during a drug incident.

After DiGiulio's murder, Anita had remarried George Marvin Jr., her third husband whom she had divorced before marrying DiGiulio. In 1993, Marvin divorced her after she accused Marvin of selling off her fortune in jewelry and furs and the $100,000 Amherst, New York home on Hopkins Road that she had purchased after DiGiulio's "death." Anita got to technically "know" the killer Miles when she was lodged in September 1994 in a jail cell one floor below his at the Erie County Holding Center, a downtown Buffalo lockup. She had been returned to Buffalo then for her post-conviction efforts to overturn her spousal-murder conviction. Unfortunately for Anita, the only "contact" she ever had with Miles was through their communication via the jail's toilet piping. Though she got lawyers to get her a marriage license for her and Miles from Buffalo's City Hall, Holding Center officials refused to grant their required permission for the nuptials.

In January 1995, Holding Center Superintendent John J. Dray told the news media that convicted killers DiGiulio, Marvin and Miles were "state property" and had to get permission from state prison officials to marry. Dray explained that "We have weddings here all the time" in his jail "but we make sure they have marriage counseling first because our female inmates are often under pressure to get married." The lovelorn Miles, who was 12 years younger than Anita, was still living in the New York State prison at Auburn at the start of the 21st Century.

In court proceedings two years after her murder conviction, Anita claimed FBI agents Coyne and Reukauf had paid her about $1,000 a year in "cash" for her informant work against Liffiton. She insisted she had remained an FBI informant through the 1980s, only being dropped following her 1990 spousal murder indictment. Granted poor-person status to appeal her murder conviction, Anita claimed during 1993 court proceedings that George Marvin had left her with "maybe $30 to $40" in her prison bank account and more than $20,000 in judgments from creditors after their abbreviated remarriage. She claimed Marvin stole her money to pay off his business debts. Former FBI informant Anita died on Jan. 21, 2003 at the age of 55 while serving her murder sentence at New York State's Bedford Hills Correctional Facility for women in Westchester County.

The FBI, which abandoned Anita like so many of its other Western New York mob informants, liked to brag publicly about how its agents had forced Magaddino to live his last years in disgrace and how he had been denied the full funeral rites of his Roman Catholic Church in 1974. But contemporary newspaper reports of the death of the Real Teflon Don described the full-blown Mass of Christian Burial he was given in Niagara Fall's St. Joseph's Roman Catholic Church and his burial in the St. Joseph Cemetery on Pine Avenue in Niagara Falls with full church pomp and circumstance on July 22, 1974.

J. Edgar and Reality

J. Edgar Hoover was both image-conscious and paranoid. He claimed to have taken over a scandal-plagued Department of Justice bureau of investigation in 1924 and personally built it into what is regarded today as the greatest law enforcement agency in the world. Hoover called one of his leading critics, Jack Anderson, a famed investigative journalist of the mid-20th Century, "a jackal," according to internal FBI memos. "This fellow Anderson and his ilk have minds that are lower than the regurgitated filth of vultures," J. Edgar Hoover said in a typed memo dated April 30, 1951, one of hundreds that existed in Anderson's FBI files. Anderson, whose famed "Washington Merry-Go-Round" column also landed him on Richard M. Nixon's presidential enemies list, caused what the Associated Press described after Anderson's death as "heartburn in Hoover's office at the FBI."

The Associated Press reports of Hoover's hatred of Anderson were documented in the FBI files which the AP obtained after a lengthy Freedom of Information Act lawsuit. The AP found that FBI officials had insisted over the years in their internal memos that

Anderson frequently got his facts wrong and that Hoover personally scribbled alongside a copy of one Anderson column preserved in the FBI secret files: "This is the greatest conglomeration of vicious lies that this jackal has ever put forth." Anderson incessantly argued that Hoover, who kept running the FBI well into his 80s, should have stepped down in his early 70s.

Even after Hoover went to that big investigation room in the sky, the paranoia of FBI officials continued, the AP found. The Post-Hoover FBI ordered an investigation of the 1972 porno movie "Deep Throat," which turned out to be the nickname W. Mark Felt, the FBI's second-in-command, used in supplying Washington Post reporter Bob Woodward "deep background" on the Watergate scandal that brought down Nixon's presidency.

With Felt's own "deep throat" adventures not revealed until he died in 2005, FBI files of the early 1970s, the AP belatedly found, indicated the agency staged an ultimately unsuccessful effort to stop the distribution of the porno movie "Deep Throat" by seizing copies of the movie and having its negatives analyzed in labs and interviewing everyone involved in the film, including messengers who delivered the movie reels to theaters. The AP found that thousands of pages of FBI documents on the porno flick had been reviewed by Felt and the FBI's top men—Hoover, L. Patrick Gray, William Ruckelshaus and Clarence Kelley. The FBI was among the many legal agencies that openly suggested the porn flick had been made with Mafia money—given the Mafia's long connections with porn—but the AP stressed that its review of the secret FBI files on the film contained no mention of mob links.

Manny Fried, a gifted American playwright, actor, college professor, factory worker and labor organizer for the United Electrical, Radio and Machine Workers, knew firsthand about FBI attitudes under J. Edgar Hoover and the problems Hoover caused people he considered public enemies. Active educationally, theatrically, intellectually and physically into his mid-90s, Fried became the central figure in a thousand page-long FBI dossier after he refused to testify before the U.S. House Un-American Activities Committee against suspected communists and communist supporters nationwide in the late 1940s and early 1950s. After being singled out by the FBI and Hoover as "the most dangerous man in Buffalo" in the 1950s, Fried received a letter from Albert Einstein congratulating him on his refusal to submit to HUAC interrogation before hot television cameras.

Fried always regretted the refusal of the FBI to obtain an indictment against him for his anti-HUAC attitude. He publicly claimed he had been confident he could have overcome FBI efforts to have him convicted and imprisoned as an alleged commie symp. Fried never forgave the FBI for that agency's unsuccessful attempt to ruin his public reputation and his career and besmirch the reputation of his beloved wife, Rhonda Lurie Fried. Mrs. Fried was a well-known Buffalo artist and heiress whose wealthy family had owned the Park Lane, once that city's top restaurant and which in its heyday hosted power lunches and dinners for some of Western New York and the nation's bigwigs in business and government. She died at 71 in 1989.

"They just couldn't stomach that I wouldn't break," the then-94-year-old Fried told a Buffalo News interviewer in September 2007 in recalling the FBI attack on him. "They felt, and properly so, that I was providing an umbrella for other people to speak," he added. Fried, once a New York City actor working off and on Broadway with John Garfield and Elia Kazan under the professional name of Edward Mann, was first called before HUAC in 1954. He refused to testify. Though the FBI has always refused to publicly comment about its active and nearly life-long pursuit of Fried, he said he learned that his FBI "terrorist" file was still getting fed information as late as 1996.

Fried, who ultimately obtained some of his massive FBI file through a Freedom of Information Act case, outlived virtually all of his Hoover-backed government enemies, fully aware of the millions of dollars in government funds spent because of Hoover's ultimately failed effort to destroy his career and his spirits. Still teaching at Buffalo State College of the State University of New York in his mid-90s, Fried said in 2007 when asked what the FBI got for all their efforts against him, "crap." Fried died peacefully at the age of 97 on Feb. 25, 2011.

8. The Don Juanabe

Magaddino's philandering son-in-law Jimmy LaDuca lived alongside the Real Teflon Don in Lewiston and drove him to the ill-fated Apalachin session in 1957. The Forest Avenue Boys knew of LaDuca's extra-marital affairs and debated the value of letting Magaddino know about the junior Casanova. But they opted against it after setting up wires at Camellia Linen which LaDuca, a one-time financial secretary and treasurer of Local 66 of the Hotel and Restaurant Employees Union, poorly ran for his father-in-law. The linen company technically was headed by Charles A. Montana, nephew of John C. Montana. Vincent A. Scro, another Magaddino son-in-law, was listed as secretary-treasurer of the linen supply concern but LaDuca had the inside dope on the Arm's operations so the Boys concentrated on him.

The Camellia tap ended up providing a treasure-trove of intelligence about Magaddino crime family plans for hits and jobs already carried out because LaDuca seemed addicted to talking about everything that was going on in the "family" as he sat in his plush Buffalo office. Through the Camellia tap, the Boys confirmed that Johnny Sacco would periodically drop off money from stolen property scores he had set up to LaDuca at the linen supply office. Whoever LaDuca called from his plush office he always referred to Magaddino, the Boys found, as "Grandpa."

Magaddino's hatred of the family of Joe Kennedy, who had screwed the mob and Magaddino personally during Prohibition, was well known. LaDuca would routinely talk about how Joe

Kennedy had used the Mafia to get his son, John Fitzgerald Kennedy, elected president. LaDuca used to talk on the Camellia tap about how Magaddino and his top officers plotted ways they could pay back Joe Kennedy by killing some or all of his beloved sons. LaDuca would talk with his pals about how plans had been discussed by "grandpa" (Magaddino), about how to get machine guns from Canada to carry out an "assignment" on the Kennedy boys. The November 22, 1963 assassination of President John F. Kennedy by Lee Harvey Oswald resolved part of the Magaddino family's desires and LaDuca was heard on the Camellia tap sharing laughs about that national tragedy with his cohorts in the Real Teflon Don's family.

In 1965, the Forest Avenue Boys began picking up talks about how Magaddino's top guns were considering using associates of entertainer Frank Sinatra to get brothers Robert and Edward "Ted" Kennedy and their then-brother-in-law actor Peter Lawford who was part of Sinatra's so-called "Rat Pack," ensnared and publicly humiliated by having them placed in compromising positions with beautiful women, either together or alone. Publicly the FBI, through Joe Griffin, claimed FBI Director J. Edgar Hoover had been alerted to that never-realized Magaddino plot through the hard work of Griffin. But in actuality Griffin became alerted to that mob scheme from the sheets he picked up on one of his frequent visits to the Forest Avenue Boys' office.

The information on that Magaddino-encouraged plot against the Kennedy family was in the secret FBI files for decades and became public in 2010 with the release of over 2,300 pages of the FBI files on Teddy Kennedy who died at age 77 of brain cancer in 2009. LaDuca's conversations on the Camellia tap revealed the Kennedy sex scheme was related directly to Robert Kennedy's bid to crackdown on mob activities while U.S. Attorney General. The get-the-Kennedys chat calmed down after Sirhan Sirhan fatally shot Robert Kennedy in Los Angeles on June 5, 1968. After that, Magaddino's Arm backed off on efforts to get Ted Kennedy because the assassinations of his brothers had led to heightened security measures by federal officials.

9. The Riots and the Mob

In 1967, Buffalo's East Side was the scene of violent street disturbances and rioting by African-Americans. In 1970, the future of Buffalo's famed Allentown Art Festival was threatened by a disturbance in a bar that spilled out onto Allen Street and affected the nearby Festival. It became clear early on through the wiretap of Camellia Linen, the Sacco wires and other wires that Magaddino and his crew did not like the slowdown in "work" those riots caused and the added number of police on the streets they had attracted.

But it was equally clear that Magaddino did not want the work of police agencies dealing with the rioters to be interfered with by his own men. The Forest Avenue Boys found the Magaddino troopers joking among themselves about Buffalo police strong-armed tactics against the largely college-age rioters during the Allentown Festival-related 1970 riot and shortly after it had been quelled. As for the 1967 uprising of blacks that virtually shut down much of Buffalo during the East Side rioting from June 26 through July 1, the Boys found Magaddino's legions loading their calls to each other with typical racist remarks about blacks.

Those race riots came as the size of Buffalo's black population had grown from about 40,000 in the late 1950s to over 100,000 by the summer of 1967. But with the black community physically split in two by the opening of the Kensington Expressway on Aug. 15, 1967, the rioting which left over 40 persons hurt, 14 by gunshots, was seen by many as a legitimate, but regrettable expression of black rage.

159

The Riots and the Mob

During the 1967 rioting, the Boys wires increased in the volume of calls they had to monitor around the clock, making good use of the cots they had installed in their home-away-from-home. During the rioting, a goodly number of businessmen contacted "Sam" Pieri and other Magaddino associates including Roy "The Fisherman" Carlise, to arrange for protection and to get repair work done on riot-damaged business addresses, with Carlise and others arranging for repair jobs and the Arm getting a cut of the contracts. Researchers at the State University of New York at Buffalo found the summertime 1967 rioting had been sparked by the dilapidated housing available to many of the city's poor, the insufficient employment opportunities for black youth and instances of physically brutal and racially-tinged actions by uniformed Buffalo police officers.

Magaddino's boys could be heard on the wires complaining about the Buffalo Mayor's historic June 29, 1967 meeting at the Michigan Street YMCA with a group of young black leaders—an event credited with bringing the rioting to a halt just days later. Magaddino's men also talked to each other about their clear distrust of blacks in general which was in line with the Real Teflon Don's refusal to get involved actively in street sales of drugs. Magaddino left those sales to black mobsters on Buffalo's East Side.

Though unrelated to the Allentown Art Festival, the 1970 disturbance came to be known as the Allentown Art Festival Riot and led to quiet but crucial negotiations in 1970 and into 1971 between the festival's organizing group, the Allentown Village Society, and City of Buffalo officials. During those talks, the Art Festival's importance to the cultural fabric of Buffalo prompted its organizers to agree to scale back the nearly carnival-like atmosphere that had come to characterize the fast growing and popular art event in the late 1960s. As the festival grew it had attracted sidewalk performances and fashion shows as well as exhibits and sales of art works.

Those negotiations led to an improvement in the quality of the art on display and created a national reputation for excellence for what had begun as a small street art show in 1958. The Forest

160

The Riots and the Mob

Avenue Boys found the Magaddino troopers kept a close watch on the Allentown riot of 1970. The riot started after police showed up on the hot evening of June 14, 1970 to deal with a fight outside Mulligan's Brick Bar on Allen Street, then a major drinking spot for young people in the Buffalo area.

The police were confronted with a noisy crowd of several hundred people fueled by alcohol. More police were called as the crowd began pelting police with rocks, bottles and bricks and the officers responded with tear gas which sent smoke billowing into the nearby festival activities still underway that evening.

While some 700 artists had been allowed to take part in the art festival by 1970, because of the riot the festival was reduced to only 450 artists the next year and after talks with city officials, festival officials limited sales to handmade work only and artists were limited to specific assigned areas of the streets. After the 1970 riot the festival was patrolled by off-duty police officers, mounted Erie County sheriff's deputies and on-duty police.

In mid-1970 Danny Sansanese called "Sam" Pieri and as they talked about the Vietnam War and related topics and the recent Allentown riot, the never-sentimental Sansanese, in what for him had to be a near-reverent tone of voice, told Pieri: "Only in America can we operate like we are."

10.   Mr. Hot to Trot

Texas attorney-politician John Bowden Connally Jr. had many political and business friends in the Buffalo, New York area, especially in the Democratic Party in the 1960s. Some of them cooled off when he became a Republican.

While manning the equipment at the Forest Avenue Boys' office in the spring of 1967, Karalus heard the voice of a prominent Buffalo-area Democratic politician speaking with Connally on the Santasiero's Restaurant wiretap. To him that confirmed long-suspected connections between the Real Teflon Don's top associates and Western New York government and political officials.

During that call, Karalus heard the Democratic politician asking to speak to the elderly Joe DiCarlo who had been branded by law enforcement in the 1930s as Buffalo's Public Enemy Number One. The politician had to patiently announce to the then-mentally deteriorating DiCarlo who he was before he mentioned that a national political figure might be coming to Buffalo sometime later in the spring of 1967 and might be in line for a local female companion during that visit.

It was made clear to DiCarlo that the celebrity, then-Texas Gov. John Bowden Connally Jr., might very well be bringing his wife "Nellie" with him on the trip to Buffalo to talk to local Democrats, but if Connally's wife did not come he wanted to make sure "a woman" would be available to provide the Texan with companionship of sorts. Karalus listened as gravel-voiced DiCarlo, who was a revered figure to the Pieri faction of the Magaddino Arm, and who rarely took calls at Santasiero's laughed and told the politician "I can get him the Barracuda," a notorious Canadian hooker who had "serviced" a number of Magaddino's legions over the years.

The Forest Avenue Boys had zeroed in on Santasiero's, a legitimate and widely-praised dining site in Western New York, because it had become clear that the Pieri faction of the Magaddino family used it as its daily meeting place. The Boys set up both a wiretap and a live wire to catch both phone calls and live talks among the Pieri family higher ups in the restaurant's back room. Karalus and the other Boys knew Elsie Rose DiCarlo, the late wife of DiCarlo, 67, was a member of the Pieri family.

In the 1930s DiCarlo had been branded by law enforcement as Buffalo's Public Enemy Number One and remained a prime Western New York mobster into the early 1960s. In fact, DiCarlo's criminal exploits were so widespread that in 1960, Jake LaMotta, the former middleweight boxing champion of the world, complained during a U.S. Senate antimonopoly subcommittee meeting run by Sen. Estes Kefauver, D-Tenn., about DiCarlo's alleged offer to fix a 1947 fight between LaMotta and Tony Janiero for a $100,000 bribe.

While "professionally" active in the Buffalo vending machine business in the early 1930s, DiCarlo was branded Buffalo's "Public Enemy No. 1" in 1934 by Buffalo Police Commissioner Austin J. Roche. During the 1930s, DiCarlo was also known as a political adviser to Magaddino prince and successful Buffalo politician and businessman John C. Montana.

John Connally (1917-1993) was an influential American politician for decades, serving as governor of Texas and as Secretary of the Navy and Treasury under Presidents John F. Kennedy and Richard M. Nixon. Connally will be remembered historically as the wounded survivor of the Nov. 22, 1963 assassination of JFK as they both rode that day with their wives in a Presidential motorcade through Dealey Plaza, Dallas about 12:30 p.m. Central Standard Time.

As Nixon's treasury secretary in the early 1970's, Connally was instrumental in creating the great U.S. inflation problems of the 1970s. Connally and Nixon pressured Federal Reserve Chairman Arthur Burns to help them end the historic Bretton Woods system of fixed exchange rates between nations. He also helped launch a currency war between nations by telling Europe that the U.S. dollar "is our currency, but your problem." Connally publicly was the devoted husband of Idanell Brill "Nellie" Connally who gave him two sons and two daughters.

He was the campaign manager for future President Lyndon Baines Johnson during LBJ's 1948 U.S. Senate campaign which featured questionable back-room maneuvers that won that election and started both men in their history-making political careers. Always the master politician, Connally got LBJ the 1960 vice-presidential slot under JFK after publicly claiming at the 1960 Democratic Party convention in Los Angeles—prophet-like as it turned out—that JFK, if nominated and elected, would be unable to serve as president for a full term because of Addison's disease and his dependence on cortisone. Though scoffed at by some in the 1960s, Connally's medical claims about JFK's Addison's disease problems were posthumously-confirmed.

At LBJ's request, JFK named Connally Secretary of the Navy in 1961, a post from which he resigned after eleven months to run for governor of Texas in 1962, serving as that state's Democratic governor from 1963 through 1969. A life-long Democrat and pal of LBJ from 1938 until the former president's death in January 1974, Connally, who had been suspected of privately favoring President Eisenhower in the 1950s, formally joined the Republican Party in May 1973. Five months later he was rumored to have been one of President Nixon's choices to replace the scandal-ridden Spiro Agnew after he resigned the vice presidency.

In January 1979, Connally announced he would be seeking the GOP nomination for President the next year but he ultimately lost out to the more popular conservative icon Ronald W. Reagan. In August 1970, Connally, working as a lawyer after his career as Texas governor ended and before he jumped politically, did come to Buffalo for what proved to be an unsuccessful lobbying effort to get the Buffalo-based Erie County Legislature re-interested in the proposed construction of a $70 million Dome Stadium in the Buffalo area under a deal his longtime friend and client, former Judge Roy Hofheinz, a former Houston mayor, had with Western

New York businessman Edward H. Cottrell for a proposed 40-year lease of the stadium.

Connally's 1970 lawyer-lobbying effort, which included a lavish dinner for members of the county's legislative body at a swank Buffalo restaurant, fell flat. Years later, after two Buffalo jury trials, the Cottrell faction ended up getting paid $10 million by the Erie County government to resolve its breach of contract suit over the failed stadium project and Cottrell moved out of the state after fighting with the Buffalo law firm which had represented him on the stadium effort.

Whether a local Democratic politician actually had been able to supply a woman for Connally or any other Democrat Party bigwigs on visits to Buffalo was something the Boys were never able to confirm. Whether or not Tex Connally sinned against his wife, the Boys, like numerous other New York State troopers through the years, knew of many an unfaithful politician statewide. Several troopers even got into trouble assisting disgraced Gov. Spitzer in his multi-state romantic odysseys.

It was never learned by the Forest Avenue Boys if a hooker was ever actually supplied for that proposed 1967 trip to Buffalo by Connally. But that call by the political operative confirmed the Boys' suspicions about the Magaddino crime family's close ties to high-ranking politicians in the Buffalo area. Whether or not Buffalo Dems ever actually succeeded in supplying a woman to Connally in 1967 or later to any other visiting Democrat Party bigwigs was something that was widely discussed by the Boys and others in local law enforcement for decades. But it was not a subject that was ever discussed publicly by Buffalo area politicians, even decades later when JFK's sexual proclivities were publicly disclosed.

11. The End

At a Buffalo Bills game at the city's War Memorial Stadium, the old Rock Pile, in late September 1972 Karalus, a diehard Bills fan since Ralph Wilson returned the city to the major leagues in 1959, had extra trouble walking. Bothered for some time by an ugly red blotch on his upper right leg and an increasing amount of pain there, Karalus found himself in agony just trying to walk up the stairs of what had been one of FDR's gifts to the city through the WPA in the 1930s. Initially called Civil Stadium and later the War Memorial Stadium, it ultimately became known as The Rock Pile.

Returning to work the day after that Bills game, Karalus got time off to drive to the nearby Millard Fillmore Hospital for what he figured would be a routine emergency room check of his leg troubles. When he got there he asked to be examined by Dr. Clarence Sanford who was busy but agreed to see him. Hours later Sanford came down and after briefly examining the leg told Karalus that what he thought was just a troublesome "blotch" was actually a life-threatening blood clot that he needed to have operated on that afternoon. Hospitalized for a week and after another week of home rest Karalus, was eager to return to work with the other Forest Avenue Boys.

To his horror when he returned to 400 Forest after being off for two weeks he found everyone shredding all their printed material and packing up equipment. Troidl told him they had been ordered to shut down the operation—with similar orders going to other special state police units across the state. The Forest Avenue

Boys were never formally told why they were being redeployed. And in the end Hank Williams, for all the work the Boys did for him, never visited the Forest Avenue office. The Boys could never figure that out, but like the good soldiers they were, marched on anyway.

Upper level State Police officials never gave the Boys a solid explanation for the closing of its successful Buffalo work, prompting years of speculation about the demise of the anti-mob effort. Two 1967 U.S. Supreme Court decisions on eavesdropping seemed to have belatedly prompted the gutting of the secret State Police units less than a decade later. Especially significant was the high court's *Berger v. New York*[4] ruling which invalidated a New York statute that authorized electronic eavesdropping without court-controlled procedural safeguards. In a case in which the law office of attorney Ralph Berger had been bugged in a bribery investigation, the nation's high court found that law in violation of Fourth Amendment constraints against warrant-less searches.

The other 1967 case was *Katz v. United States*[5] in which the high court extended Fourth Amendment protection against unreasonable searches and seizures to include protecting persons from telephone booth wiretaps done without a court warrant. That blew an FBI gambling conviction in California. The Berger case hit directly at undercover police operations in New York State and was centered on the failure to allow periodic judicial review of ongoing secret operations. Attorneys for Ralph Berger challenged wiretap evidence in his case before the Supreme Court in 1967 as they fought his conviction for trying to secure a liquor license through a bribe which was a crime under provisions of a new New York State law. The nation's high court overturned the lower court rulings, agreeing with Berger's attorneys that the state law was overly broad and trespassed by failing to require that lawmen precisely describe the place to be searched and the persons or things that they wanted to seize, including the nature of any conversations they sought to be "seized," in violation of Berger's Fourth Amendment rights.

---

[4] 388 U.S. 41 (1967).
[5] 389 U.S. 347 (1967).

The End

Starting with the Berger decision, the high court began applying constitutional mandates on electronic surveillance by law enforcement. Also in 1967, the high court expanded that mandate in the case of Charles Katz of Los Angeles who had been convicted of transmitting electronic betting information across state lines by telephone. The evidence against Katz had been telephonically harvested by FBI agents who had, without a search warrant, installed a listening device on a telephone booth Katz was known to use.

The high court agreed with Katz' attorneys that "the evidence used against him at trial was gathered illegally and therefore should have been ruled inadmissible by the trial judge." The court voted 7-2 to overturn Katz's conviction, a landmark holding that Fourth Amendment protections cover all areas in which there is a reasonable expectation of privacy, including on a telephone. Justice Stewart in the majority opinion on Katz wrote:

> "The Fourth Amendment protects people, not places. What a person knowingly exposes to the public, even in his own home or office, is not a subject of Fourth Amendment protection. But what he seeks to preserve as private, even in an area accessible to the public, may be constitutionally protected."

The Katz ruling which the Forest Avenue Boys followed carefully, created a new legal atmosphere in which electronic surveillance was acceptable only as far as it conformed to Fourth Amendment holdings.

COINTELPRO Spells Doom

What seems a more likely rationale for the abrupt closure of the Forest Avenue operation and others like it state-wide was the public disclosure in 1971 of the massive COINTELPRO (Counter Intelligence Program) venture that J. Edgar Hoover had launched in

1956 against the operations of the Communist Party of the United States and communists in America in general.

Thanks to J. Edgar Hoover's heavy-handed use of intelligence gathering to further his own political, personal and professional ambitions—which heightened the political paranoia of the Democrats—much U.S. intelligence gathering was severely constrained until the start of the radical Islamic terrors launched at the end the 20th Century.

Though the Forest Avenue Boys had routinely picked up references to Cheektowaga, New York, and its government officials in many of their Magaddino wires and live hookups, subsequent investigations sparked by the tantalizing Boys' data led only to six years of expensive criminal investigations of the Cheektowaga town government and the indictments of some of Cheektowaga's top elected officials including Town Supervisor Daniel E. Weber, long-time Cheektowaga Town Justice Joseph E. Pyszczynski and long-time Cheektowaga Police Chief of Detectives William G. Graham. But all but three of those town officials were ultimately cleared after criminal trials in Buffalo, New York in the mid and late 1970s.

And only one of the three convicted Cheektowaga officials spent any time behind bars—two months—and that only because he was arrested for patronizing one of the Cheektowaga gambling dens initially launched by Magaddino's boys years earlier. Though the Buffalo Evening News took credit in the 1970s for sparking the massive and expensive investigations of alleged corruption in the Cheektowaga town government, there were those in law enforcement who wondered what might have been accomplished had the Forest Avenue Boys remained together and electronically delved deep into Cheektowaga doings, as they had done with the world of Stefano Magaddino. The thinking was that possibly more meaningful criminal cases could have been developed and hundreds of thousands of dollars of taxpayer funds could have been better deployed in fighting serious Erie County crime in the 1970s.

In October 1973—long after the Forest Avenue Boys were shut down, the first of two Erie County grand juries launched a full-court press on the Cheektowaga town government. The second grand jury had to be empanelled because procedural problems had tainted the work of the first panel. Lacking the court-sanctioned talents of the Forest Avenue Boys, in 1973 Erie County, NY, District Attorney Edward C. Cosgrove and his Organized Crime Bureau launched a wide-ranging criminal investigation of Cheektowaga government affairs, taking full advantage of the investigative talents of the State Police Bureau of Criminal Investigation.

After 15 cartons of Cheektowaga Town Court records were seized through grand jury subpoenas in late December 1975, long-time Cheektowaga Town Justice Joseph E. Pyszczynski, who was not a lawyer, publicly denounced what he called "the Gestapo tactics" of the police and the district attorney's office. "There was no need for this," the judge said. "Those are public records and we would have been glad to furnish them without this disruption of court business," he added.

Five months after the seizure of those records, Pyszczynski, then 59, and a town judge since 1952, was indicted for allegedly taking money to fix drunken driving cases, becoming the first sitting judge in Erie County, New York history ever indicted. The first grand jury panel in what some came to call the Mini-Watergate government scandals of Cheektowaga voted to disband in November 1974 after lawyers challenged its operation.

In January 1975, Erie County District Attorney Edward C. Cosgrove corrected the first panel's problems and launched a special grand jury targeting Cheektowaga, obtaining indictments of Town Supervisor Weber, Town Justice Pyszczynski, the Police Department's Chief of Detectives Graham, town councilmen Felix T. Wroblewski, Joseph R. Obstarczyk, Raymond J. Wasielewski, Donald A. Halicki, town Sanitation Supervisor Edward J. Banko, former chairman of the Cheektowaga Democratic Party and former town Plumbing Inspector Carl Trafalski.

Cheektowaga Police Detective Lieutenant Richard F. Golembiewski, whose departmental promotion had been pushed by Weber, was indicted on bribery charges by the special grand jury on Dec. 30, 1975. Less than 24 hours later, he fatally shot himself in the stomach in his home, literally hours before he was to have been arraigned, thus dying a legally innocent man.

The End

Supervisory-level officials in the District Attorney's office refused to let District Attorney Cosgrove's investigators (who by then included Karalus) house Golembiewski at a swank Buffalo hotel where they had planned to press him to rat on others in the town government and police department.

In June 1975, one of the two bribery indictments against Wroblewski—as a co-defendant of Halicki and Trafalski—was thrown out by State Supreme Court Justice Frederick M. Marshall on procedural grounds. In September 1975, a State Supreme Court jury in Buffalo convicted both Halicki and Trafalski of bribery and on Nov. 19, 1975, State Supreme Court Justice Marshall, historically a tough sentencing judge, placed both on probation for three years and fined Halicki $1,000 and Trafalski $2,000.

In October 1975, State Supreme Court Justice Frank J. Kronenberg dismissed the first of Weber's official misconduct and bribe-taking indictments and in May 1977 State Supreme Court Justice Jerome B.E. Wolff dismissed a similar pay-off case against Weber, Wroblewski, Obstarczyk and Wasielewski.

In December 1975, another State Supreme Court jury in Buffalo convicted Banko of official misconduct and theft of services. Though Justice Marshall on Jan. 20, 1976 ordered Banko to serve an 8-month local jail term and pay a $1,000 fine, he didn't surrender until June 6, 1977 because of a protracted set of appeals by his attorneys. While appealing that conviction, Banko was arrested in April 1977 at an old Magaddino gambling den in Cheektowaga and charged with patronizing illegal gambling. He was released from jail on Aug. 9, 1977.

In 1976, former Cheektowaga assistant plumbing inspector Norbert E. Skibinski was convicted of perjury for lying during his grand jury testimony but all he got was a judicial rebuke.

A Buffalo jury on April 27, 1977 took about four hours before finding Pyszczynski, then 60 and a town judge since 1952, not guilty of taking bribes to "fix" two 1975 drunk driving cases even though Joseph P. McCarthy, then deputy district attorney of Erie County, New York, and later the supervising judge of all criminal courts in Western New York, told the jury the case "goes to the very heart of the criminal justice system." Pysczynski was represented at that

The End

1977 trial by John W. Condon Jr. and Joseph V. Sedita—two of Buffalo's top criminal defense lawyers.

On Oct. 5, 1978 Pyszczynski, by-then retired from the bench, saw New York State Supreme Court Justice Jerome B.E. Wolff of Buffalo—in the midst of a second jury trial—dismiss the last of the bribe-receiving cases, one that stemmed from a 33-year-old former prostitute's claim that she had sex with the Cheektowaga judge three times in 1971 to have him dismiss her latest speeding ticket. At the urgings of Justice Wolff, the Erie County district attorney's office launched a perjury probe against that admitted former prostitute, Darlene Kowal and Richard Gorski, a Cheektowaga building contractor and long-time friend of Pyszczynski, who gave authorities conflicting claims about the alleged sex deal. Gorski first claimed he had arranged the sex and then denied knowing anything about such a seamy affair.

In February 1979, that perjury probe was unceremoniously abandoned by the Buffalo prosecutor's office with no one being charged with perjury and the massive probe of Cheektowaga government doings quietly closed. Pyszczynski died an innocent man at the age of 72 in June 1989.

Before Daniel E. Weber died in May 1998 at the age of 76, the former Cheektowaga police detective sergeant ended up presiding over the town's most explosive period of growth including the development of the Walden Galleria which established Cheektowaga as the area's premier shopping destination. Danny also became a national figure with unsuccessful campaigns in the 1980s at the state and national levels trying to repeal automobile seat belt laws.

District Attorney Cosgrove declined public comment following Weber's second acquittal in 1977. Through the years, many local lawmen wondered what would have happened with the Cheektowaga government probes had the Forest Avenue Boys been allowed to refocus their wires on that town government.

Redeployed after the 1972 close of the Forest Avenue operations, the Boys speculated about what if any role their old ally Hank Williams played in the unit's closing. The death of the State Police anti-mob units, many of the Boys felt, seemed to have been fostered by actions in the 1970s of the Democratically-controlled Congress' Church Committee which unwittingly tied the hands of the nation's national intelligence operations behind their backs.

The Church Committee's antics were compounded in the 1990s by the Clinton-era decision of Deputy U.S. Attorney General Jamie Gorelick who will historically be known as the creator of the "Gorelick Wall" which barred anti-terror investigators from inter-agency cooperating and in effect prevented government access to the computer files of violent terrorists.

The "Gorelick Wall" seemed to many in Washington prior to the horrid 9-11 Twin Towers incident of 2001 to be a logical follow-up to the work of the Church Committee in the 1970s. The 9-11 horror showed the tragic consequences of the growing political correctness that set the stage for the Islamist terrorism of the end of the 20th Century and into the 21st Century.

In the end, most of that political-correctness was really the consequence of the damage done to the nation's political structure and its law enforcement operations by Richard Nixon's ill-conceived—and as it turned out politically unnecessary—Watergate burglary of the Democratic National Committee headquarters in the Washington D.C. office complex on June 17, 1972 which ended in Nixon's Aug. 9, 1974 presidential resignation.

As the Wall Street Journal editorialized on Aug. 25, 2009, the Obama Justice Department's decision to set up a special prosecutor's inquiry for a reexamination of CIA interrogations of Islamic terrorists after the Sept. 11, 2001 tragedy was just like the Church probes of the 1970s that forced the hasty shutdown of the highly successful Forest Avenue Boys operation and others like it nationally. The Journal complained that once again the Democratic Party cared more about settling political scores against fellow Americans than fighting the war on terror.

Though the Forest Avenue Boys never have been given credit publicly for successfully penetrating into the inner workings of Magaddino's well-disciplined mob army, their efforts set the stage for the ultimate dismantling of the Real Teflon Don's vast crime empire.

The End

With the Boys just a faded memory, the Magaddino empire ended up being divided into smaller criminal enterprises controlled by former Magaddino lieutenants.

Index

Index

Index

Index

Index

Index

New York Joint Legislative Committee on Government Operations, 26

New York State Inspector General's Office, 3

New York State Organized Crime Task Force, 26

New York State Police, 1, 9, 10, 11, 16, 29, 30, 31, 38, 39, 43, 58, 68, 85, 102, 106, 122, 123, 126, 135, 137, 143

New York Telephone, 35, 36, 121, 125

Newton, Wanye, 93

Niagara Mohawk Power Company, 76

Nicoletti, Benjamin, 39, 103, 104, 110, 111

Nixon, Richard M., 11, 107, 154, 155, 164, 165, 174

O'Hara, Anthony J., 148

Obstarczyk, Joseph R., 171, 172

Olmsted, Frederick Law, 29

Omnibus Crime Control Act of 1968, 27

Operation Emerald, 141, 143

Orwell, George, 117

Oswald, Lee Harvey, 158

Palascak, Eddie, 3, 47, 126, 139

Pan-American Exposition of 1901, 53

Papalia, John, 89, 95, 96

Parness, Gregory, 50, 58, 59, 61, 108

Passero, Patsy, 103, 104, 111

Pataki, Governor George, 146

Paterson, Gov. David A., 68

Pawlak, Eddie, 2, 34, 42, 125

Pellicano, Dr. Victor L., 101, 104, 105

Perrello Family, 76

Perry, Fred, 89

Petrie, Patrick, 39

Phelan, Andrew, 102, 105

Picasso, 58

Pieri, Sam, 4, 5, 7, 32, 38, 40, 41, 43, 47, 48, 49, 50, 60, 63, 65, 88, 89, 108, 112, 113, 143, 160, 161, 163, 164

Pinelli, John, 152

Pitt Petri store, 47

Policastro, Sgt. Peter, 13

Power City Distributing Company, 76

President's Commission on Law Enforcement and Administration of Justice, 99

Presley, Elvis, 149

Profaci, Joe, 18, 21, 25, 81

Prohibition, 73, 76, 91, 157

Przbyl, Stanley, 80

Puglese, Sam, 103, 104, 111

Purks, Alver, 89

Pyszczynski, Justice Joseph E., 170, 171, 172, 173

Index

Index

Index

Acknowledgments

The author relied on extensive interviews with George Karalus, particularly for the Introduction and Chapters 2, 3, 4, 5, 6, 8, 9, 10 and 11. Other retired state troopers interviewed include Tony Direnz (Ch 5), Joseph Benenati (Ch. 1), Ken Troidl (Ch. 4), and Edgar Croswell's son, Robert (Ch 1).

Additional sources include:

Chapter 1—The Mother of All Raids—The Associated Press (including Croswell quotes), The Buffalo Courier Express, The Buffalo Evening News, later the Buffalo News, Wikipedia, the report of The Pennsylvania State Crime Commission released in February 1969, Niagaratimes.com, Little Italy Niagara Museum, Niagara Falls, NY., Niagarafallsreporter.com; U. S. Senate Committee on Governmental Affairs, Permanent Subcommittee on Investigations: Profile on Organized Crime Mid-Atlantic Region, 1983. Buffalo and Erie County, NY, Public Library; Buffalo and Erie County, NY, Historical Society; The Associated Press; Time Magazine; Buffalo homicide detective Eddie Gorski; Chicago Sun-Times newspaper; Jack Anderson and his Washington Merry-Go-Round nationally syndicated newspaper column; "I Heard You Paint," book written by Frank "The Irishman" Sheeran; The Binghamton, NY, Press and Sun-Bulletin newspaper; The Binghamton, NY, Sun newspaper; Providence, Rhode Island, Journal-Bulletin newspaper; The Grey Rider and PBA Trooper publications of the New York State Police, Sept-Dec. 2007. The

Miami (Florida) Herald newspaper; The Niagara Falls, NY, Reporter.

Chapter 2—The Office: Courier-Express articles: April 21, 1967; June 30, 1967; Jan. 8, 1968; Dec. 5, 1968; Dec. 6, 1968; Sept. 7, 1969 and June 3, 1970. Courier Express photo reprinted with permission of the E.H. Butler Library at Buffalo State College; Photo of Buffalo Psychiatric Center grounds in Buffalo, New York courtesy of the Buffalo Psychiatric Center, with special thanks to Sue Joffe, director of public information and volunteer services; Daniel DiLandro, Buffalo State College archivist and special collections librarian; E.H. Butler Library, Buffalo State College, Buffalo, NY.; The United Press International wire service reports on mob revenue in the early 1970s; Sid Birzon—Buffalo News articles; Anthony Sisti—Buffalo News articles, including Matt Gryta coverage of the estate case pitting one Sisti daughter against the other Sisti daughter; Buffalo News articles, Courier-Express May 6, 1970, May 12, 1970; New York Times Aug. 17, 1921; Dan Weber— Buffalo News, May 5, 1998; Courier-Express April 5, 1976, May 17, 1977.

Chapter 3—The Real Teflon Don: background on Magaddino and the Mafia—Wikipedia, AP, and www.lacndb.com; Big Korney—Courier-Express, Sept. 11, 1932, June 10 1944; Alberto Agueci—Wikipedia, AP; Magaddino and the Kennedys—Buffalo Courier-Express, Buffalo News, George Karalus; Ontario Police Commission—AP; Joe Bonanno—Wikipedia; Magaddino legal battles—Buffalo News, Courier Express May 5, 1970; John Camilleri—Buffalo Evening News, May 9, 1974; Courier-Express; Good Killers Gang—Niagara Falls Reporter.

Chapter 7—The FBI and Its Enemies: Mob Nemesis: How the FBI Crippled Organized Crime, by Joe Griffin, published by Prometheus Books; Lee Coppola quote, Buffalo News Oct. 21, 2005, Jack Anderson on The Washington Merry-Go-Round column May, 3, 1970 and May 9, 1970, Courier-Express May 4, 1971. Federal court battles—Buffalo News, Courier-Express, AP, Courier-Express May 4, 1971, Sept. 2, 1971, Dec. 12, 1971; Hoover and COINTELPRO—Wikipedia; Operation Emerald—Buffalo News, including Matt Gryta reporting; Sal Martoche/Hide in Plain

Sight—Buffalo News, Courier-Express, AP; William Sciolino—
Buffalo News, Courier-Express, George Karalus; Manny Fried—
Buffalo News, AP.

Chapter 8—The Don Juanabe: Courier-Express, Buffalo
News.

Chapter 9—Riots and the Mob: AP, Buffalo News, Courier-
Express.

Chapter 11—The End: Buffalo News, Oct. 7, 1978, Oct. 7,
1978, Feb. 2, 1979, April 28, 1977; Courier-Express, April 28, 1971,
May 5, 1998, June 4, 1971 and Matt Gryta reporting.

About the Author

Matt Gryta is a legendary court and crime reporter in Buffalo, New York. He has covered the courts for thirty-six years and personally witnessed many of the legal battles described in this book. He wrote this book because of the desire of George Karalus to chronicle the hard work he and his teammates performed in dogging the Magaddino's crime family.

Gryta is a former college newspaper editor-in-chief and has been a Buffalo News staff reporter for over four decades. From 1970 through May 1971, Gryta was a U. S. Army war correspondent in Vietnam. A 1969 graduate of the State University of New York College at Buffalo (B.A. English), Gryta was editor-in-chief of The Record, Buffalo State's student newspaper in both his sophomore and senior years. He was a college intern for two summers at the Buffalo Courier-Express newspaper and joined the staff of the then-Buffalo Evening News (later The Buffalo News) in the summer of 1969, from late in the summer of 1970 through May 1971.

Gryta, as a draftee who came into the army with professional experience as a police reporter and general assignment reporter for The News, became a U.S. Army war correspondent in Vietnam and NCO in charge of reporters and photographers. Returning to the states, Gryta completed 10 graduate level courses in the Economics Department at the State University at Buffalo (UB) but did not complete course work for a master's degree. He has been a professional journalist in Buffalo for over four decades.

Made in the USA
Lexington, KY
01 November 2012